Praise for *Lean Customer De*

"*Cindy has done us a great service.* Lean Customer Development *shines the light on the discipline of developing a clear understanding of the customer. By understanding who the customer is, what their real needs are and developing clear hypotheses; product, design, and engineering can design, build, and test what customers really want. This frees teams to focus on the business of bringing the best experiences to life instead of a product nobody wants. Whether you are a startup or a large enterprise you need to develop this discipline and this way of thinking about the customer. I recommend this book.*"

Bill Scott—Senior Director UIE, PayPal

"   *drives home the case for maintaining a continuous dialog with our   omers. This book is chock full of actionable steps to make the most   ou   ery conversation, user test, and feedback session. She opens up the   rese   process encouraging teams to build a shared understanding of their   needs and the validity of their hypotheses. Make sure you add this   t   step-by-step guide to your arsenal of product development tools.*"

Jeff Gothelf—Author, *Lean UX*

"*Co   ies are learning that the only competitive advantage is the ability   to m   continuous learning and iteration part of their culture. For many   la   rganizations, including Microsoft, this means re-learning how to   enga   ith customers as partners.* Lean Customer Development *offers a   view   ow companies of any size can practice deep customer learning in parallel with product development.*"

Adam Pisoni—Corporate Vice President, Microsoft

"*T   s a daunting book. It's so packed with concrete steps, hard facts, and p   n techniques that it removes any excuses you might have around buildin   e right product for the right market. When I finished it, the first thing I wanted to do was go read it again. The second thing was to get out of the building and test five startup ideas. It's that good.*"

Alistair Croll—Founder, Solve for Interesting

995003291 1

Lean Customer Development

Building Products Your Customers Will Buy

Cindy Alvarez

Beijing · Boston · Farnham · Sebastopol · Tokyo

Lean Customer Development

by Cindy Alvarez

Copyright © 2014 Cindy Alvarez. All rights reserved.
Printed in the United States of America.

Published by O'Reilly Media, Inc., 1005 Gravenstein Highway North, Sebastopol, CA 95472.

O'Reilly books may be purchased for educational, business, or sales promotional use. Online editions are also available for most titles (*oreilly.com/safari*). For more information, contact our corporate/institutional sales department: (800) 998-9938 or *corporate@oreilly.com*.

Editor: Mary Treseler	**Cover Designer:** Mark Paglietti
Production Editor: Kara Ebrahim	**Interior Designers:** Ron Bilodeau and Monica Kamsvaag
Copyeditor: Jasmine Kwityn	
Proofreader: Becca Freed	**Illustrator:** Kara Ebrahim
Indexer: Bob Pfahler	**Compositor:** Kara Ebrahim

June 2014: First Edition.

Revision History for the First Edition:

2014-05-08	First release (hardcover)
2014-07-08	Second release (hardcover)
2014-11-14	Third release (hardcover)
2015-06-05	Fourth release (hardcover)
2016-04-22	Fifth release (hardcover)
2017-08-30	Sixth release

See *http://www.oreilly.com/catalog/errata.csp?isbn=0636920016724* for release details.

Nutshell Handbook, the Nutshell Handbook logo, and the O'Reilly logo are registered trademarks of O'Reilly Media, Inc. *Lean Customer Development* and related trade dress are trademarks of O'Reilly Media, Inc.

Many of the designations used by manufacturers and sellers to distinguish their products are claimed as trademarks. Where those designations appear in this book, and O'Reilly Media, Inc., was aware of a trademark claim, the designations have been printed in caps or initial caps.

Although the publisher and author have used reasonable care in preparing this book, the information it contains is distributed "as is" and without warranties of any kind. This book is not intended as legal or financial advice, and not all of the recommendations may be suitable for your situation. Professional legal and financial advisors should be consulted, as needed. Neither the publisher nor the author shall be liable for any costs, expenses, or damages resulting from use of or reliance on the information contained in this book.

ISBN: 978-1-492-02374-6

[LSI]

Contents

Foreword

Steve Blank's ideas are so well known today that some may not realize that when he first self-published *The Four Steps to the Epiphany*, he was very much a voice in the wilderness. Steve, with whom I've been fortunate to work as an investor, mentor, and friend, was courageous enough to call for bringing the rigorous approach of product development to the business and marketing functions of startups—long before mainstream entrepreneurs and VCs caught on; in so doing, he inspired many of us to rethink our beliefs about startups. He called that theory Customer Development.

Now that these ideas have taken hold well beyond the San Francisco Bay Area and become an integral part of the Lean Startup movement, it's high time to revisit them and share some of the success stories, tips, and tricks from the trenches. It's fitting that Cindy Alvarez, an early Lean Startup evangelist, has drawn upon her experience at early-stage startups and Fortune 500s alike—most recently, for Microsoft as Director of User Experience at Yammer—to write a nuts-and-bolts guide for a new generation of entrepreneurs.

The word "entrepreneur" may bring to mind the image of college kids working on some new technology in a garage, but my meaning is a little different. A startup includes any human enterprise designed to create a new product or service under conditions of extreme uncertainty, and an entrepreneur is anyone tasked with ushering in that change. Whether they're building a company in their garage, working for a VC-backed startup, or trying to drive innovation at an enterprise or nonprofit, what all entrepreneurs share is the need for a process that converts the raw materials of innovation into real-world success.

Companies both large and small have been drawn to a more nimble, iterative approach to innovation and growth, but as they soon discover, doing so requires a different way of interacting with current and prospective customers. The goal of any startup is to figure out the right thing to build as quickly as possible, and the Lean Startup is a set of practices for helping entrepreneurs increase their odds of success. How do we know if we're building the right thing? How should a cross-functional team work together? How do we hold people accountable? These are the questions the Lean Startup methodology was designed to answer.

Customer Development is different from traditional marketing research methods. While those techniques can help us understand customer needs and preferences, and take us inside the user experience to show us how customers use a product or service, this goes a step beyond—using scientific experimentation to put what we've learned to the test. Our goal is to not simply understand customer behavior, but to learn *how* to change customer behavior and build a sustainable business.

The process involves running many tests at microscale in order to get the engine of growth turning, so that a startup can achieve hypergrowth. This is one of the reasons the methodology is so challenging: it requires people to work in a truly cross-functional way to synthesize what they've learned. It means working hand-in-hand with colleagues from marketing, engineering, operations, and customer service—in other words, everyone. Engineers and scientists without traditional marketing or sales backgrounds now find themselves hearing straight from the customer's mouth what he thinks about the product. People on sales teams who've been used to presenting final products recognize that the feedback they receive in sales calls can be of tremendous value to the innovation process. People in customer support positions are empowered to better meet customer requests rather than simply trying to put out fires.

But even after they've prepared themselves to speak to customers or potential customers, many who are new to the Lean Startup methodology have plenty of questions: "How can I convince people to spend their time talking to me about a product we haven't even finished building?" "How do we get information from our best customers without potentially alienating them?" "If a customer cannot place an order, how can we assess whether we're on the right track?"

Cindy provides answers to those questions and more, offering techniques to help entrepreneurs stay grounded in reality even in the discovery phase of the process: rather than relying on what customers tells us they would like to do in the future, she provides strategies for finding out how customers actually behave. "Actually changing behaviors, spending money, or learning something new has a cost," she explains. "You need to figure out the difference between want and will, and uncovering that difference requires discipline in how you talk to your target customers."

Often, this means thinking creatively about how to turn an exploratory customer interview into an experiment. While working with a large bank that insisted on asking customers, "Are you concerned with the security of your financial information?" all 10 customers Cindy spoke to answered "Yes." This wasn't giving her the insights she needed so she switched gears, telling one customer he would only be entitled to the $50 gratuity if he shared his mother's maiden name and Social Security number. "Without hesitation, the man grabbed a ballpoint pen and reached for my sheet of paper," Cindy writes. "I stopped him before he could write anything, but my point was made. Very concerned about security...until $50 was on the line."

A word of caution to anyone embarking on the Lean Startup journey: If you think you know what's important to your customers, you're in for a big surprise. Whether you work at a large corporation or a scrappy startup, whether your enterprise is hoping to build the next big thing or your startup is learning how to deal with hypergrowth, whether you build consumer-facing apps or large industrial engines, this difficulty unites every one of us.

The Lean Startup process won't give you all of the answers, and neither will *Lean Customer Development*. Instead, we hope these techniques will help you challenge your assumptions as quickly as possible so that you can build a lasting company that serves customers well.

Eric Ries
San Francisco
April 14, 2014

Preface

We have guesses about what's good for the user, but we're mostly wrong. No matter how good you are, you're mostly wrong.

—Adam Pisoni, CTO of Yammer

In a startup no facts exist inside the building, only opinions.

—Steve Blank

In 2008, at the startup I was working for, my manager dropped Steve Blank's *The Four Steps to the Epiphany* on my desk. "You have to read this book," he said. "It's brilliant and we need to learn from it."

Blank wrote about the failures (and successes) he'd experienced in two decades and eight technology companies. Through his experiences, he recognized a process that was missing from startups, which he called "customer development." In reading his book, I recognized both mistakes that I'd made and mistakes I'd observed in companies around me. We were not verifying that we were building something customers would buy. Too often we substituted our internal industry and product knowledge for customer input.

I also recognized some of the techniques in the book. I had already been using them in my career—not because I'm as smart as Steve Blank, but out of necessity as a user experience professional working in companies with a lot of uncertainty, no budget, and no dedicated team.

It was with *The Four Steps* in my head that I walked into my first meeting with one of our early customers. It was an easy meeting; they liked us and nodded in approval as my manager talked about our upcoming product release. As the hour drew to a close, people around the table made the universal gestures of a meeting wrapping up: snapping laptops shut, gathering papers, fishing business cards out of their wallets.

I asked a question: "I know we've shown you what's coming in the next release—but I'm curious... If we could add anything to the product, how could we make it more useful and valuable for you?"

I wasn't really expecting an answer.

The project manager on the customer team paused. "Well..." she said, "your recommendations widget gets us more engagement, which makes us more money, which is great. But not all of the pages on our site are monetized equally. Some pages are 10 or 20 times more valuable to us, and we have specific page-view commitments for them. If you could specifically help us promote *those* pages, you would help us make *a lot* more money."

As we walked out the door, my boss said, "I can't believe we've been working with them for almost a year and we never asked that question."

Over the next couple of weeks, I talked to more customers. I listened as they described how they worked with business partners, what helped them make money, and who made purchasing decisions. What I learned from those conversations spurred us to change our product and *triple* our price.*

This short conversation is a great example of what I call lean customer development. Just one question posed to a customer. Just one shift in perspective—away from building a better product and toward building a more successful customer. It led us in a new direction, saved us time, and brought in a lot more money.

It's a simple formula. Learn what your customers need, and use that knowledge to build exactly what they're willing to pay for.

---

* Wouldn't it be great if this anecdote ended with the company reaching unprecedented heights of success? It didn't. The product pivot that came from this conversation did directly boost revenues and win additional customers, but failure to understand the business model ultimately doomed the company. If only I'd been able to read this book back then! I would have realized that we were dependent on a key partner—advertising companies—that probably saw the bottom falling out of their market before we did.

Who Is This Book For?

If you are a startup founder in the San Francisco Bay Area, this book *is not* for you.

Why? Because you've probably not only read Eric Ries's *The Lean Startup* and Steve Blank's *The Four Steps to the Epiphany* (or at least tried to get through it), but also many of the other books in the O'Reilly Lean Series. More importantly, the Bay Area is full of speakers, bloggers, and peers who embrace change and experimentation. Even your prospective customers have an above-average tolerance for the new.

This book *is* for the entrepreneurial product person who isn't in such a supportive environment.

Maybe you've read *The Lean Startup*. You're thinking, "This sounds great—but *how* do I actually do it?"

You may work in a startup or in a large organization where you think you can't get away with using tactics that work for startups.

I built my career in the Bay Area, but I've spent most of my time working with people like you. I've worked in startups where our customers were in conservative or change-averse industries like finance, publishing, healthcare, legal, or construction. In 2012, the company I work for, Yammer, was acquired by Microsoft. Since then I've been evangelizing lean and training Microsoft employees on how to adapt to a faster, more hypothesis-driven culture.

In other words, I feel your pain and I can show you how to apply these tactics, whether you're working at a startup or in an established company.

This book is for product-centric people in technology or offline businesses, service businesses, big companies, conservative industries, and even heavily regulated industries. This book is for:

- Product managers, designers, and engineers who want to increase their next product's chances for success

- Product-centric people in large organizations who are struggling to help their organizations move faster and work smarter

- Entrepreneurs seeking to validate a market and product idea before they invest time and money building a product that no one will buy

In this book, I've provided lots of examples to help you see customer development in action. You'll find a variety: examples from startups and examples from established companies. There's also variety in the kinds of products: products aimed at consumers, products sold to businesses, software products, services, and even food products.

Because the simple approach to customer development that I present can help you no matter what your product focus or the size of your organization, I'll ask you to read all the examples, not just those that fit your industry. The principles you'll learn will be worth your time.

Who Can Practice Customer Development?

What do you need in terms of background and skills to practice customer development? All you need are three qualities:

Ruthless pursuit of learning

> It's uncomfortable to ask questions that might prove you (or your boss) wrong. It's also essential to success.

Comfort with uncertainty

> Customer development isn't predictable; you don't know what you're going to learn until you start. You'll need the ability to think on your feet and adapt as you uncover new information.

Commitment to accepting—and escalating—a reality check

> Some of your team's assumptions will be proven wrong. You'll need to convince people to change their minds and their plans based on what you learn.

If you've got these three qualities, this book will give you the background to start practicing customer development immediately. You'll also gain an understanding of the social psychology behind the tactics I show you (i.e., *why* they work). Because every company is different, you'll want to adapt the techniques from this book to make them work for your situation. Knowing *why* they work will empower you to do just that.

You might also wonder how many people you need to do customer development. In fact, even one person can drive this change.

If you're the founder of a new startup, you may be that person.

In my experience, even in organizations with multiple people practicing customer development, one person coordinates and consolidates what everyone is learning. That's why throughout this book I'll be talking straight to you.

How Does This Book Fit into O'Reilly's Lean Series?

This book is part of a series of books inspired by Eric Ries's *The Lean Startup: How Today's Entrepreneurs Use Continuous Innovation to Create Radically Successful Businesses*. Each book expands on one of the ideas in Ries's book and provides a deeper guide to putting those ideas into practice.

You don't need to have read *The Lean Startup* or any of the other books in this series to read this book.

What Is Lean, Anyway?

The term "lean" originally comes from manufacturing, specifically from Toyota. It stresses eliminating waste from processes and making sure the end product is something that the customer wants.

Customer development can be considered part of lean, because it helps you streamline your product development process and ensures that you create something that the customer wants.

Because customer development is a core element of the lean startup, you will find mentions of it in other books in the series. However, *lean customer development* is unique in that it focuses entirely on how to get out there and start practicing customer development today. It's also unique in that it is explicitly directed at both startups *and* mature, existing companies, in recognition of the fact that lean tactics are now being used in companies of all sizes and types. You don't have to work in a startup to use this book—in fact, enterprise companies may well need it more!

Why I Wrote This Book

Customer development is critical to success, but grossly underutilized. Here are the top four reasons I believe this is so:

- We're biased toward our own great ideas.

- We feel that our industry knowledge entitles us to skip validating those ideas and jump to creating products.*

- We don't know how to find customers before we have a product.

- Most of the information to date on this topic is long on telling you why you need customer development, but short on telling you how to do it. As a result, most people don't know where to start.

---

* It doesn't matter that you've got a team of smart people who know the industry. There is no shortage of failed products built by great teams with strong track records and industry expertise. As Ries puts it, "Most likely, your business plan is loaded with opinions and guesses, sprinkled with a dash of vision and hope."

I don't want to see more companies make the same mistakes I and so many others have made!

This book tells you exactly what to do, how to do it, and why you should do it, so that you reduce your risk and accelerate your progress from idea to profitability.

What You'll Learn

This book offers a practical education in customer development. Figure P-1 illustrates an overview of the process and serves as a guide to where each step is covered in this book.

In Chapter 1, "Why You Need Customer Development," we'll arm you with the facts you need to overcome initial resistance from your organization about doing customer development.

In Chapter 2, "Where Should I Start?", we'll get you started with identifying assumptions, writing a problem hypothesis, and mapping your target customer profile.

In Chapter 3, "Who Should I Be Talking To?", we'll describe how to find your target customers and get them to talk with you.

Chapter 4, "What Should I Be Learning?", details the types of questions that effectively identify customers' existing behaviors, pain points, and constraints—and explains why these questions work.

Chapter 5, "Get Out of the Building," gives you a play-by-play for successful customer interviews. You'll learn how to introduce yourself, get people talking, and get beyond shallow answers to detailed, thoughtful facts about customer behavior and needs.

Chapter 6, "What Does a Validated Hypothesis Look Like?", shows you how to synthesize the valuable insights you've gained and use them to drive product and business decisions.

Chapter 7, "What Kind of Minimum Viable Product Should I Build?", describes the different kinds of MVPs and what situations each one works well in.

In Chapter 8, "How Does Customer Development Work When You Already Have Customers?", you'll discover how to set expectations appropriately and reassure customers. For those of you in large enterprises, in conservative or regulated industries, or constrained by long sales cycles, this chapter will reassure you that you can make customer development work in your organization.

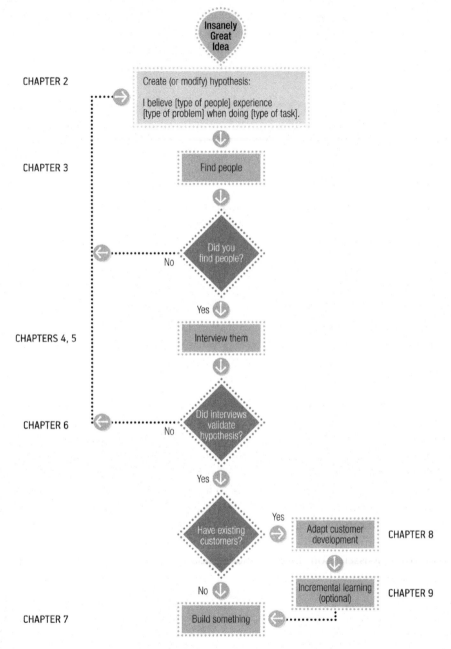

Figure P-1. Customer development is a continuous process for learning and validating your hypotheses

Chapter 9, "Ongoing Customer Development," gives you strategies for fitting customer development into your everyday routines and piggybacking on existing customer interactions to continuously gain insights. By the end of this chapter you'll have new ideas for creating more opportunities to talk with your customers.

The appendix, "Questions That Work," offers tried-and-true questions to ask and describes when to use each question, as well as what you can expect to learn from asking it.

A Word of Thanks

First of all, thanks to the people who trusted me to try out all of the tactics and questions in this book on our customers over the years: Hiten Shah, Peter Hazlehurst, Tim Sheehan, Jim Patterson, and Pavan Tapadia.

Justin Lin deserves a lot of credit for figuring out exactly how much to nag me to keep writing. Serena Lin was less subtle: "When you going to be done writing, Mommy?"

Thanks to Maureen Be, Vanessa Pfafflin, Grace O'Malley, Jamie Crabb, and Priya Nayak—my amazing research team at Yammer—who have been refining these ideas and using them to make our product teams and our product better.

So many of you were helpful in various ways: making introductions, offering suggestions, reviewing outlines, vetting my references, and recommending me for the speaking engagements that inspired me to write this book. Thank you to all of you, and especially to Henry Wei, Trevor Owens, Bhavik Joshi, Andrew Wolfe, John Petito, Eugene Kim, Sarah Milstein, and of course Eric Ries and Steve Blank. Thanks to my editors: Mary Treseler, who greenlit this book, and Deb Cameron, who helped bring shape and structure to a bunch of ideas and footnotes. To my reviewers, Tristan Kromer, Marcus Gosling, Robert Graham, Phillip Hunter, Chuck Liu, Matthew Russell, Tom Boates, and especially Lane Halley. Your thoughtful suggestions and criticisms helped evolve this book in a great direction.

CHAPTER 1

Why You Need Customer Development

It is humbling to see how bad experts are at estimating the value of features (us included). Despite our best efforts and pruning of ideas, most fail to show value when evaluated in controlled experiments. The literature is filled with reports that success rates of ideas in the software industry are below 50%. Our experience at Microsoft is no different: only about a third of ideas improve the metrics they were designed to improve.

—Ronny Kohavi, Partner Architect at Microsoft

Nature hath given man one tongue but two ears, that we may hear from others twice as much as we speak.

—Epictetus

Customers are what make a product successful.

Without customers willing to buy, it doesn't matter how good or innovative or beautiful or reasonably priced a product is: it will fail.

It makes no sense, then, that we spend most of our time and effort optimizing our *product* development process. What about *customer* development? Shouldn't we invest at least as much time in understanding our customers, their needs and pain points, and how to deliver solutions to them?

Customer development is an approach for doing just that.

It's a way to reduce your business risks by challenging your assumptions about who your customers are, what they need, and why and how they buy.

By applying the scientific method to learning about your customers, you can help confirm that you're on track to a business model that works and a product that people want to buy.

Sounds great in theory, right?

But theory is useless if you can't put it into practice. That's why I've written this book—because I've worked with, mentored, and spoken to hundreds of companies who love the lean ideas and principles but struggle to make them work.

The First Challenge Is Inside the Building

Customer development is a big change for most organizations.

To many people, customer development sounds like saying, "Hey! You know that expertise that we've amassed over decades of experience, dozens of products, and millions of customers? Let's shelve it and start from scratch."

Of course that's not what we're saying. But as a pragmatist, I recognize that it's difficult to correct a mistaken first impression. If your team doesn't understand what customer development is and how it enhances (rather than replaces) your competencies, it'll be far more difficult to get started.

Customer development is admittedly the new kid on the block. Everyone knows about the role of product development, marketing, customer support, and even user research in an organization. But customer development? You're likely to encounter some skepticism.

Unless your team has been exposed to lean startup conferences or Steve Blank's work, you may find yourself having to sell customer development to your organization before you can really get started.

This chapter takes a step back, explaining what customer development is (and isn't), why you need it, and who can do it. It also offers responses to some common objections.

What Is Customer Development?

So let's back up a minute and talk about definitions. What is customer development? What does it replace? What does it *not* replace?

The term *customer development* is meant to parallel *product development*. While everyone has a product development methodology, almost no one has a customer development methodology. And the truth is, if you don't learn what customers really want, you're at a very high risk of building something that no one wants to buy.

Customer development is a hypothesis-driven approach to understanding:*

- Who your customers are
- What problems and needs they have
- How they are currently behaving
- Which solutions customers will give you money for (even if the product is not built or completed yet)
- How to provide solutions in a way that works with how your customers decide, procure, buy, and use

You probably have ideas or intuitions about all of these. Let's identify what those really are: guesses. Let's make it sound a bit better and call them *hypotheses*. Those hypotheses may be around forming a new company, building a new product, or even adding new features or capabilities to an existing product.

Everything you do in customer development is centered around testing hypotheses.

What Is Lean Customer Development?

You may have heard of customer development. So what's the difference between "customer development" and "lean customer development"?

I call my approach to customer development "lean customer development." I'm using "lean" as a synonym for pragmatic, approachable, and fast.

Lean customer development takes the heart of Steve Blank's ideas and renders them into a simple process that works for both startups and established companies. It's what I write about on my blog, speak about at tech events, and teach when I mentor companies.

---

* If you've read Steve Blank's *The Four Steps to the Epiphany*, you'll recognize that this is not his original definition of customer development. Blank defined the four steps as customer discovery, customer validation, customer creation, and company building.

But *The Four Steps* was written explicitly for startups, and Blank is very clear that "a startup is not a small version of a big company." Having worked for over a decade in startups and now being a part of Microsoft, I completely agree. They are very different beasts!

Since customer development works for both startups and larger enterprise companies, I've proposed a broader definition that works for companies of any size, at any stage of maturity.

Lean customer development can be done by anyone who speaks with customers or prospects. It works whether you're a startup founder with no product and no customers, or at an established company with numerous products and customers. Now that I've explained my perspective on lean customer development, from here on out, I'm going to talk simply about customer development.

In my experience across multiple companies and in mentoring startups, every hour spent on customer development has saved 5, 10, or even more hours of writing, coding, and design (Figure 1-1). That doesn't even include the harder-to-measure costs such as opportunity cost, snowballing code complexity, and eroding team morale from working hard on features that no one ends up using.

Figure 1-1. Talking to customers saves time and money

Customer development starts with a shift in mind-set. Instead of assuming that your ideas and intuitions are correct and embarking on product development, you will be actively trying to poke holes in your ideas, to prove yourself wrong, and to invalidate your hypotheses.

Every hypothesis you invalidate through conversations with prospective customers prevents you from wasting time building a product no one will buy.

Lean customer development is done in five steps:

- Forming a hypothesis
- Finding potential customers to talk to
- Asking the right questions
- Making sense of the answers
- Figuring out what to build to keep learning

If your hypothesis is wrong or even partially wrong, you want to find out fast. If you can't find customers, you modify your hypothesis. If customers contradict your assumptions, you modify your hypothesis. Those course corrections will lead to validating an idea that you know customers want and are willing to pay for.

What Customer Development Is Not

There are as many misunderstandings about what customer development isn't as about what it is. Let's clear those decks right now.

Customer Development Is Not Just for Startups

When *The Lean Startup* was published in 2009, many companies were slow to embrace the ideas it introduced. "*We're* not a startup," they replied.

Although Eric Ries uses the word "startup" in the title of his book and Steve Blank wrote specifically about customer development as it pertains to startups, startups are not the only companies that benefit from customer development. Startups certainly have a higher degree of uncertainty than mature companies; they are still searching for a business model, a distribution strategy, a customer base.

But larger, more mature companies also can't assume that their models will remain static. Markets and technology change. In addition, larger companies often find it difficult to shift attention and resources away from profitable lines of business in order to explore new markets and areas of innovation—leaving them ripe for disruption. (Kodak, which I write about in Chapter 8, enjoyed over 100 years of success before missing the boat on digital imaging and declaring bankruptcy in 2012.)

Customer development, with its focus on small-batch learning and validation, can promote internal innovation. Intuit, for example, has launched multiple products using customer development—including SnapTax and Fasal. General Electric is using lean principles. So is Toyota, the New York Department of Education, and the White House's Presidential Innovation Fellows program.

Much of the content in this book is applicable for readers from early-stage startups, massive established companies, and anything in between. When a section is more useful for one audience than the other, I have called that out.

Customer Development Is Not Product Development

Product development answers the question "When (and what) can they buy?"

Customer development answers the question "*Will* they buy it?"

Product development is the process of building a new product or service and (one hopes) bringing it to market. Start with a concept, define the requirements, build the requirements, test the near-finished product, refine it, and launch it.

How you develop a product varies tremendously based on the methodology your organization follows (e.g., Waterfall, Agile, Scrum, etc.). What all product development methodologies have in common is the desired outcome: *a completed product* for customers to buy.

But what if the product you build is not a product that customers will buy? Is "product" the biggest risk your team faces? What about market risk? As Marc Andressen said, "Market matters most. And neither a stellar team nor a fantastic product will redeem a bad market."*

With customer development, you are building your customer base *while* you're building a product or service that solves their specific problems. Customer development doesn't replace product development; it's a second process that you do in parallel with product development.

If you've done customer development alongside product development, you don't need to wait until your product is launched to know whether customers will buy. You'll know, because you will already have beta customers, evangelists, and paying customers.

Customer development and product development are two independent activities, and both are necessary to maximize your company's chances for success.

Customer Development Does Not Replace Product Management

Some folks object, "Well, what's left for product managers to do?"

Customer development does not replace product vision. Talking to your customers does not mean asking them what they want and writing it all down. Product management requires a disciplined approach to gathering

---

* *http://web.archive.org/web/20070701074943/, http://blog.pmarca.com/2007/06/the-pmarca-gu-2.html*

information from a variety of sources, deciding which pieces to act upon, and figuring out how to prioritize them.

Customer development simply adds two components: a commitment to stating and challenging your hypotheses and a commitment to learning deeply about your customers' problems and needs.

Customer development does not provide all the answers. Although it can replace many of your assumptions with actual information, it still requires a disciplined product manager to decide which pieces of information to act upon, how to prioritize them, and how to take what you've learned and turn it into a feature, product, or company.

Customer Development Is Not User Research

Your company may be conducting user research already. That doesn't mean you're practicing customer development.

Customer development does borrow from many of the techniques that have served user researchers well for decades. But the context, the practitioners, and the timing are very different.

User researchers often describe their work as "advocating for the user." It is, unfortunately, still viewed in many companies as optional, something you *should* do because it delights customers.

Customer development is "advocating for the business." It's not something that you *should* do because it makes customers happy. It's something you *must* do to build a sustainable business where people open their wallets and pay for your product or service.

Why You Need Customer Development

Most new products (and companies) fail. The odds are against you. Around 75% of venture-backed startups fail.* Anywhere from 40% to 90% of new products fail to gain significant market adoption.†

---

* You'll hear varying numbers. The National Venture Capital Association, for instance, estimates that only 25% to 30% of venture-backed startups fail completely. But the discrepancy may be due to different definitions of failure. Harvard Business School senior lecturer Shikhar Ghosh estimates that 30% to 40% of high-potential startups end up liquidating all assets—a failure by any definition. But if a startup failure is defined as not delivering the projected return on investment, then 95% of VC companies are failures, Ghosh said (*http://www.inc.com/john-mcdermott/report-3-out-of-4-venture-backed-start-ups-fail.html*).

† The number varies across product categories. Highly innovative products fare even worse. For more information, see *http://www.cob.unt.edu/slides/paswan/MKTG4320/freepdfgrab.pdf*.

But surely, we think, we will be the exception. We like to think of building products as an art—something guided by our creativity, intuition, and intellect. We all know that there are good product managers (and designers and engineers and strategists) and mediocre ones. Maybe that's what makes the difference between a failed product and a success?

Unfortunately not.

Universally, we're just not very good at building products and companies solely based on creativity, intuition, and intellect. It's not just a startup problem, either: in 1937, the companies that made up the S&P 500 had an average life expectancy of 75 years; recently that number has dropped to just 15 years.*

On a smaller scale, we're not as good as we think we are, either. Most of our ideas don't increase value for customers or companies—Microsoft estimates that only around one-third of their ideas improve the metrics they are intended to improve. Amazon tests every feature and fewer than 50% work; Yammer's numbers are roughly the same. Netflix and Intuit don't claim any higher proportion of successes.†

The truth is that it doesn't matter how much companies research, how well they plan, how much money they spend, or how smart their employees are: the odds that they'll avoid big mistakes are worse than a flip of a coin.

---

* "What went wrong? [startup guru John Hagel III] argued that American companies and their leaders were essentially not prepared for a move away from a corporate model of 'knowledge stocks'—developing a proprietary product breakthrough and then defending that innovative advantage against rival companies for as long as possible—and toward a more open and collaborative business model that he called 'knowledge flows.' The problem, he said, is that because of the increasingly global nature of business competition, the value of a major proprietary breakthrough or invention erodes in value much more quickly than in the mid-20th century" (http://knowledge.wharton.upenn.edu/article.cfm?articleid=2523).

† Numbers from a Microsoft ThinkWeek paper (http://ai.stanford.edu/~ronnyk/ExPThinkWeek-2009Public.pdf).

Not Just Software

I may be citing a lot of software companies, but the benefits of risk reduction and course correction are even greater for other businesses. Lines of code are far cheaper and faster to change than manufacturing setups, supplier contracts, and compliance approvals.

There's limited opportunity to regain trust in a service that disappointed your customer, and no opportunity to alter a physical product once it's in a customer's hands.

For the makers of KRAVE jerky, it was critical to understand how customers defined a premium snack food (no nitrates, no artificial ingredients) before committing to a recipe and starting mass production.

For Romotive, a company that makes smartphone robots for learning, it was critical to understand the environments that their robots would be moving in. "The robot has to have good mobility and traction on carpets, hardware floors, or over grates. Also, kids drop things! A lot of what we've learned about how these robots will live has influenced our hardware decisions," says marketer Charles Liu.

How Do We Improve Our Odds?

In part, we improve our odds by embracing the idea that building products is a systematic, repeatable process. There are tools that you can use, regardless of your company's size, maturity, or industry, to help increase your chances of success. Customer development is one of those tools.

By practicing customer development as a parallel process in conjunction with product development, you can greatly maximize your learning and reduce your risks.

If you've read *The Lean Startup*, you'll recognize the diagram on the left side of Figure 1-2 as the Build-Measure-Learn feedback loop. It's meant to describe how your organization should be continuously learning and adapting based on the new information you get from measuring results and learning from customers. The diagram on the right side, the Think-Make-Check loop, is a variation coined by LUXr CEO Janice Fraser.

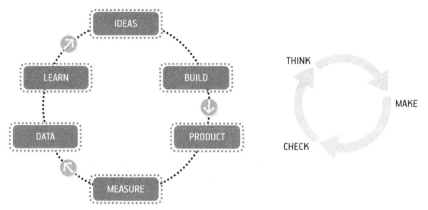

Figure 1-2. The Build-Measure-Learn feedback loop
Ries described in The Lean Startup *(left) and the Think-*
Make-Check cycle that Janice Fraser describes in her
thinking on lean UX (right)

What's the difference? Just the starting point. You don't need to start with the Build phase—in fact, doing so is often an expensive way to experiment.

Customer development is an important part of the Think phase. It allows you to explore and iterate during the cheapest phase of development—before any code is written or mockups are created. Customer development gives you the necessary information to build the best possible first guess, which you will then validate.

I've talked about learning more and reducing risk—those are valuable gains, but they don't feel very tangible. What else will you gain from practicing customer development?

- You'll get a richer picture of your customer and your competition (not just companies and products but established habits and routines)
- You'll uncover new opportunities for differentiation
- You'll *reduce* the amount of product you need to build

Yes, that's right: you'll almost certainly end up writing less code! This is a consistent benefit I've heard from development teams: the ability to make their minimum viable product (MVP) even smaller. By talking to customers, you'll frequently find that customers really want only two of the five features you think you need (and they may want one more you hadn't thought of).

Everything You Know Is Wrong

Well, not quite. But as humans, we are subject to a lot of cognitive biases: our brains take shortcuts that prevent us from seeing the world the way it truly is.

We tend to operate as though we are usually right, and we interpret neutral or ambiguous evidence as supporting our beliefs rather than challenging them. This is called confirmation bias, and it's responsible for a huge percentage of product failures.

Confirmation bias is our innate tendency to pay more attention to information that confirms our beliefs.* We're more likely to ignore or downplay facts that contradict our beliefs, or interpret subjective information in a way that favors what we want to believe.

We don't do this because we're bad or egotistical people; it's what our brains naturally want to do. Unfortunately, it leads us to subtly sabotage ourselves: to ignore the person whose feedback contradicts one of our main assumptions or to dismiss a person as a dumb user because he doesn't understand or value our product.

Overcoming cognitive biases is difficult. What helps is simply writing things down. By objectively documenting our assumptions, as well as the input we get from customers, it is easier to spot the discrepancies and notice when the evidence is proving us wrong.

---

* *http://en.wikipedia.org/wiki/Confirmation_bias*

In 2009, I was lucky enough to join a startup called KISSmetrics, which had Eric Ries as an advisor. KISSmetrics had previously built two unsuccessful versions of a web analytics product. For both versions, the company had spent many months in development, only to launch and realize that their product wasn't solving a problem that customers needed to solve.

KISSmetrics CEO Hiten Shah hired me to help them build the third version of their product in accordance with lean startup principles. This time, they wanted to build a version that would allow the team to get the maximum amount of validated learning about customers with the least amount of effort. My first task: figure out what should be in that MVP.

I spent the first month of that job on the phone, on IM, and drinking coffee with people. I was shocked to find that:

- So many people were willing to talk to a total stranger who didn't even have a product
- The features that most people requested were far more ambitious than their current behaviors and tool usage
- We'd be able to cut our product scope *in half* for our initial beta

The third version of KISSmetrics was built in a month.* It was missing tons of features and included a lot of code that made our CTO cringe. But it was enough to provide value to customers and enough for us to glean valuable insights that shaped the future direction of the product.

Answering Common Objections

I'll assume that you're convinced of the value of customer development having read this far. But how can you respond to people who are not so convinced? Table 1-1 offers tactics for responding to common objections.

Table 1-1. Responding to common objections

Objection to customer development	Your response
If we talk about our future product ideas, what's to stop someone from stealing them and launching them before we do?	First of all, we're not telling people our product idea. That would bias what we hear from them. We're talking to people who have a problem we hope we can solve. We're talking to them about their problem, and how they've tried to solve it so far.
What if they figure out what our idea is and then steal it?	It's *extremely* unlikely that anyone we talk to is in a position to act upon our ideas. But even if someone was, a great idea is nothing without great execution. By talking to customers and understanding their needs and what makes them buy, we'll be more likely to release a superior product.

---

* KISSmetrics CEO Hiten Shah talked about the failed first two versions of KISSmetrics at the first Startup Lessons Learned conference (now called The Lean Startup conference): *http://www. slideshare.net/hnshah/kissmetrics-case-study-about-pivots*.

Objection to customer development	Your response
What if we get bad press coverage because of this?	For startups: We're not at a place yet where anyone wants to give us press coverage of any kind. For enterprise: We're talking to an extremely small sample size, and we will set expectations appropriately. If it makes you feel more comfortable, we can ask prospective customers to sign non-disclosure agreements (NDAs). But this hasn't been a problem for GE, Intuit, or Microsoft… so it's unlikely to be a problem for us.
How will we find people to talk to? We don't have a product or customers yet.	We'll have to figure this out once we have a product, won't we? Come on, we know we're solving a specific problem for a specific kind of person—we just need to figure out where those people are online or in the real world. (See Chapter 3.)
What if this damages our relationships with existing customers?	Customer development is actually an opportunity to build stronger relationships with some of our customers. We'll choose those most likely to be receptive, and we'll set expectations appropriately. (See Chapter 8.)
If we do customer development, what's left for the product manager to do?	Customer development doesn't mean asking customers what they want and building exactly that! It's a process for gathering information, and it will require a skilled product manager to prioritize that information and figure out what and how we respond to it. Customer development is just another tool to help our product managers do their jobs more effectively.
We already do market research and usability testing. How is this different?	Customer development gives us information on how individual customers behave and buy. We don't get that from market research—it's more high-level, covering aggregate populations. We don't get that from usability testing—that just tells us whether someone can use our product, not whether they would buy it. Market research and usability testing may still be valuable, but they serve different purposes from customer development. Customer development is the best low-effort way to confirm our assumptions about who our customer is, what he needs, and what he'll buy.

Objection to customer development	Your response
How can we justify taking time away from building our product?	If a few hours of customer development helps us discover that even one of our assumptions is flawed, that's likely to save us weeks of coding and design time. Plus, doing customer development doesn't mean we can't make progress on the product. We can—and should—do both in parallel.
Shouldn't we let product managers, engineers, and designers focus on what they're good at: building the product?	If the team wants our product to be successful, they should understand the problem the product is trying to solve! But I understand that not everyone wants to spend all day talking to customers. We can involve folks in a very lightweight way so that they have a half-hour or an hour's exposure to customers without killing their productivity.

Let's Make This Work

In the next nine chapters, I'll show you exactly how to do customer development. I'll cover specific exercises, tools and templates, sample questions, and methods that you can immediately put into practice. I'll also provide some necessary background in behavioral economics and social psychology research—not because I love theory, but because understanding *why* a technique works will help you adapt it to suit your needs and the needs of your organization.

You don't need experience in market research or user research or even in talking to customers at all—all you need is an open mind and a willingness to challenge your ideas to make them stronger.

Next Step: Get Started

As I mentioned at the beginning of this chapter, *everything you do in customer development is centered around testing hypotheses.* Now it's time to start forming those hypotheses. In Chapter 2, you'll jump into exercises that help you identify your assumptions, the problem you're solving, and who your customer is.

Key Takeaways

- Every hour spent on customer development saves 5, 10, or even more hours of writing, coding, and design.

- Your goal is to invalidate your assumptions about what customers want, so that you can focus on building what they will actually buy.

- Customer development works for companies of all sizes, not just startups.

- Customer development doesn't replace product development. You are building your customer base while you're building a product or service that solves their specific problems.

- Customer development informs product management, which then decides what to build and how to prioritize features.

- You have to work to disprove your assumptions. Cognitive bias causes you to naturally see what you want to see (what confirms your assumptions) and tune out what you don't want to see (what invalidates your assumptions).

CHAPTER 2

Where Should I Start?

It's too easy to think we know our customers from all the meetings, phone calls, and reports we've read about them. To deeply understand how people actually use our products we need to go to where they work, where they play, and where they live.

—Braden Kowitz, lead designer at Google Ventures

I'm not writing it down to remember it later;
I'm writing it down to remember it now.

—Slogan for Field Notes notebooks

The amount of customer development you do will depend on whether you're attempting to validate a brand-new business idea, launch a new product to an existing customer base, or simply add or change features in an existing product.

But whether you plan on spending a few hours or a few weeks on customer development, you'll get the most out of your time by starting with a strong foundation.

To get that foundation in place, I want you and your team to do three exercises that will take less than an hour total to complete (Figure 2-1):

- Identify your assumptions

- Write your problem hypothesis

- Map your target customer profile

I recommend these three exercises because it's fairly easy to get your team members to participate regardless of whether they embrace customer development or are actively skeptical. It's hard to argue with "Let's make sure everyone understands what we're trying to achieve and how."

For some of you, these exercises may feel redundant. Surely everyone on the team already knows our working assumptions and what we're trying to achieve, right? You'd be surprised at how often that *isn't* true, even for highly collaborative teams.

These exercises are a fast and effective way to form initial hypotheses on how you're going to provide value and make money and who you're going to target. If you want more rigor (and are willing to invest more effort up front), you may want to complete a Business Model Canvas instead of or in addition to these exercises (see "The Business Model Canvas" later in this chapter for details).

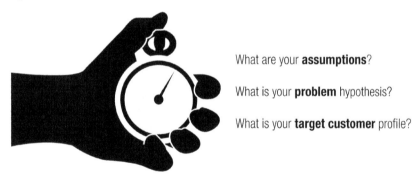

What are your **assumptions**?

What is your **problem** hypothesis?

What is your **target customer** profile?

Figure 2-1. All you need to start answering these questions is some time and something to write with

Exercise 1: Identify Your Assumptions

Along with your product ideas, you have dozens of assumptions. There are things you believe to be true about how your customer thinks and acts, what he is capable of, and how he makes decisions. There are things you believe to be true about how you will produce your product, the resources and partners you may work with, and how you will get your product in front of customers.

You should spend some time identifying your assumptions whether you're starting a brand-new company, launching a new product to existing customers, or adding a new feature to an existing product. If you are just starting, you may feel like these assumptions are wild guesses; if you are working in an existing enterprise, you may feel highly confident that your assumptions are correct. Either way, you must identify your assumptions explicitly in order to be able to rigorously validate them.

Ready? Set? Go!

Get some pens and sticky notes and set a timer for 10 minutes. Then start writing, as quickly as possible, your assumptions about your customers, product, and partners. If you're doing this as a group exercise (and I hope you are), don't stop and discuss during the 10 minutes. The point isn't to write what you think is correct; it's to unlock the mostly unspoken assumptions in your head.

Here is a list of prompts to help you bring your assumptions to the surface:

- Customers have _____ problem
- Customers are willing to invest _____ to solve this problem
- Stakeholders involved in using/buying this product are _____
- Partners involved in building/distributing this product are _____
- Resources required in building/servicing this product are _____
- If customers did not buy/use our product, they would buy/use _____
- Once customers are using our product, they will gain _____
- This problem affects our customers _____
- Customers are already using tools like _____
- Customer purchasing decisions are influenced by _____
- Customers have [job title] or [social identity]
- This product will be useful to our customers because _____
- Customers' comfort level with technology is _____
- Customers' comfort level with change is _____
- It will take _____ to build/produce this product
- It will take _____ to get X customers or X% usage

This is a list of triggers to help you get started. Once you start identifying assumptions, it will become clearer what other beliefs you hold about how you plan to build, design, distribute, and create value with your product.

You may think that there's no way you're going to be right about your cost structure or key partners on day one, and that's probably right. Steve Blank likes to quote boxer Mike Tyson on prefight strategies: "Everybody has a plan until they get punched in the mouth."*

It's not important that you're right; it is important that you write down your assumptions. They serve as a critical reminder to you that you haven't yet proven or disproven them.

After you've finished, if you've done this as a group, spend another 10 minutes clustering similar sticky notes. For example, put all the sticky notes around "Customers have X problem" together. You're likely to see assumptions that contradict each other, even within a small group. Finding these internal misalignments will help your product even before you start talking to customers!

You will want to refer back to your assumptions throughout your customer development process—at first as a reference for finding customers and thinking of questions to ask, and later to annotate them as you collect evidence that validates or invalidates them.

Now that you've completed a brain dump of your assumptions, it's time to come up with a simple, provable hypothesis.

---

* This is far more entertaining than Blank's original version, "No business plan survives first contact with a customer" (*http://bit.ly/1iXUUjB*).

The Tyson quote is explained here: *http://bit.ly/1iXUY2C.*

The Business Model Canvas

Another tool that can prompt you to identify your assumptions is the Business Model Canvas (Figure 2-2).*

Students who take one of Steve Blank's entrepreneurship classes at Stanford, UC Berkeley, or online at Udacity begin by sketching out a business model canvas for their business idea and updating it each week based on what they've learned.

Most organizations I've talked with use the canvas more as an inspiration than something to religiously update each week. If you're new to customer development, the canvas is a helpful reminder that you've likely made assumptions about a number of areas beyond just your product and primary customer.

---

* You can get poster-sized canvas images to print at *http://www.businessmodel-generation.com/canvas*.

There are alternate versions. Ash Maurya, entrepreneur and author of *Running Lean*, remixed Alex Osterwalder and Yves Pigneur's work to produce his version, the Lean Canvas (*http://practicetrumpstheory.com/2012/02/why-lean-canvas/*). You can find the Lean Canvas at *http://leanstack.com/*.

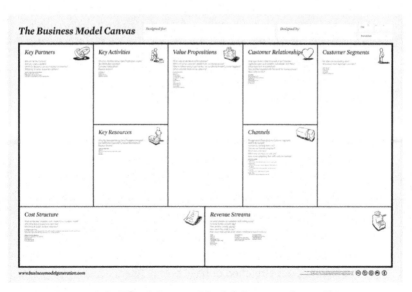

Figure 2-2. The Business Model Canvas, from Oster-walder and Pigneur's book Business Model Generation

Exercise 2: Write Your Problem Hypothesis

Next, you'll write your problem hypothesis. This is the hypothesis that you will either validate or (probably) come back and revise.

Write your hypothesis in this form:

> I believe [type of people] experience [type of problem] when doing [type of task].

or:

> I believe [type of people] experience [type of problem] because of [limit or constraint].

Let's break it down. Your hypothesis needs to consider the five journalistic questions: who, what, how much, when, and why.

The type of person who experiences the problem—that's *who* you need to talk to. The type of problem that they're experiencing—that's the *what*, *how much*, and *when* that you'll need to find out. The type of task or constraint—that's the *why* that you'll need to understand.

Turning Products into Hypotheses

Already got a product? You may need to work backward to come up with your hypothesis. Think about the value you're providing, the audience who will potentially get that value, and why they need it. It might help to look at these hypotheses for existing products (which, I will admit, I made up; I have no idea if this is how the owner of these products would have characterized them):

- I believe that [tech operations teams] experience [wasted time and budget] when [predicting network bandwidth usage for their growing companies]. (Amazon S3)

- I believe [small businesses] experience [inability to grow their businesses] because [traditional email marketing platforms are too expensive and complicated]. (MailChimp)

- I believe that [parents] experience [fear about infant health] when [putting infants to sleep]. (Halo SleepSack)

- I believe [professional men] worry about [potential embarrassment] because [they don't have time to buy new underwear when the old ones get stretched or have holes]. (Manpacks)

If you have a product and customers, the most direct approach is simply to observe your customers!

Travel site Hotwire started with simple, scrappy listening labs—setting up in an on-site conference room and using Skype to communicate with friends of Hotwire employees. That allowed the team to identify the biggest pain points with the existing site. Hotwire uses what's called "opaque booking"—the customer pays a lower rate, but the name of the hotel isn't revealed up front. Because the customer isn't sure which hotel she'll get, it's especially important that she know where her prospective hotel is located.

Watching people struggle with the Hotwire site made it clear that they were struggling with geographical orientation. "They didn't know where these results would sit on a map," explained interaction designer Karl Schultz. The more savvy customers opened up Google Maps in a separate browser window; the less savvy prospective customers simply abandoned the site.

It was easy for the Hotwire team to form an initial hypothesis: [Travelers] are unable to [feel confident enough to complete a hotel booking] because [they can't figure out where their prospective hotels are located].

You want to make each learning cycle as rapid as possible. Each time you're wrong, you'll learn a little bit about why you were wrong, which helps you make a more educated guess the next time.

Write down your hypotheses and save them. You'll be referring to them again later.

Go Narrow

One quick tip: All this talk about hypotheses being wrong might lead you to suppose that you should start with something broad and general. After all, if you don't know much yet, why would you rule anything out?

In short, speed. The more narrow your focus, the faster your progress.

I state this explicitly because it's the opposite of what most people expect. You might wonder, "If I start with a very specific profile, isn't it more likely I'll guess wrong?"

Yes, but that's OK.

If you start with a very broad scope, you'll find a huge amount of variation between individuals. You may end up doing 20, 30, or more interviews and still not be sure if you're on the right path.

Think about it this way: is it faster to disprove that cats like water or that animals like water?

Exercise 3: Map Your Target Customer Profile

What does your customer look like, and what about her abilities, needs, and environment make her more likely to buy your product?

Chances are, you don't know exactly what your customer looks like. Even if the problem is one you're experiencing personally, it's hard to know who else is part of your target market.

Start by asking questions like:

- What is the problem?

- Who is experiencing this problem?

You probably identified a fairly broad audience, such as moms or working professionals. That may represent the audience that will *eventually* be interested in your product. But anyone familiar with the technology adoption lifecycle knows that not all of these people will be ready to buy or use your product on day one. You need to find and focus on those day one people, found on the left side of the innovation adoption lifecycle (Figure 2-3).

In working with a number of product teams, I've found that it's usually difficult to know where to start. One exercise that works well is to draw opposing traits on a spectrum (Figure 2-4) and ask two questions: is this relevant? And if so, where do we think our customer sits on this spectrum?

What makes a trait important is how it influences the customer to make decisions. For example, if you believe that your target customer values cash, that conflicts with offering a full-featured product at a premium price.

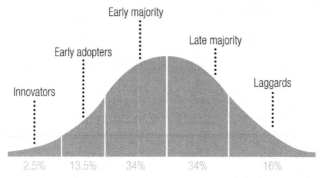

Figure 2-3. The innovation adoption lifecycle: only inno-vators and early adopters are willing to try imperfect or incomplete solutions—those who wait for trusted solu-tions aren't useful customer development interviewees*

Figure 2-4. The traits spectrum shows a sample of traits that may positively or negatively influence a customer's willingness to solve his problem with your solution

The advantage of the traits spectrum is that it's visual. I recommend sketch-ing these out on a whiteboard with your entire team and soliciting input as you go. In my experience, doing this helps bring a more diverse set of thinkers into the process. Engineers, designers, and salespeople who might not read a long document will participate in a short whiteboard exercise.

The following lists should get you started, and then you can add criteria specific to your industry or vertical.

If you're targeting consumers, you might want to start with some of these traits as a jumping-off point:

- Cash versus time
- Decision accepter versus decision maker

---

* Source: *http://en.wikipedia.org/wiki/File:DiffusionOfInnovation.png*

- More control versus more convenient
- Low-tech versus tech-savvy
- Replaces frequently versus long-term purchaser
- Values adventure versus values predictability
- Enjoys highs and lows versus prefers consistency

If you're targeting business customers, you might want to start with some of these traits:

- Low-tech versus tech-savvy
- Low autonomy versus high autonomy
- Conservative corporate culture versus progressive corporate culture
- Risk-averse versus risks are rewarded
- Values stability versus values recoverability
- Prefers turnkey solutions versus prefers best-of-breed pieces

You can create a surprisingly full target customer profile using only opposing traits like this. To round it out, you may also wish to ask a few general questions:

- What does this person worry about the most?
- What successes or rewards does this person find the most motivating?
- What is this person's job title or function?
- What social identity (teenager, mom, frequent business traveler, retiree, athlete, etc.) would this person use to describe herself?

Some of you will wonder why you've done all this work up front before you start talking to people. Others will wonder why you need to talk to people when it was so easy to come up with very plausible customer profiles on your own!

What this profile does is give some structure to the conversations you're going to have. Once you've been through a few interviews, you'll be able to take each assumption and say "this seems true—*and here's why*" or "this seems false—*and here's why*."

Demographics Aren't Customers

You'll notice that nowhere in here have I mentioned traditional marketing demographic information such as age, gender, race, household income, or marital status.

That's because such information is a poor substitute for what you really want to know: Is someone going to buy this? Who are they? What are the factors in their life that will drive them to buy this product?

Duncan Watts, principal researcher at Microsoft, writes: "When marketers think about their demographic, they actually construct stories about [invented] individual people.... In reality you have this very diverse population of people who have all kinds of needs and incentives and who are also interacting with each other in ways that are hard to anticipate. [Invented] stories ... paper over all of that complexity, effectively replacing the whole system with a single 'representative individual' and then try to reason about that person's behavior as if she were an actual person. It's a big error."

Once you have a product and you're shipping thousands or millions of units, demographic information may reveal some interesting patterns, but that's a long way off at this point.

Resist the urge to look for large amounts of generic information, such as analyst reports, census data, or market surveys. What will help you build an amazing product starts with highly specific, detailed, and passionate information—in small amounts.

Next Step: Find Your Target Customers

Now that you have a target customer profile, you're ready to start looking for customers to talk to. Chapter 3 helps you explore who they are, where you can find them, and how to reach out to them and schedule interviews.

Key Takeaways

- Spend time as a team writing down your assumptions so you can validate or invalidate them. Even if you think everyone is in alignment, they probably aren't.

- Write your problem hypothesis: I believe [type of people] experience [type of problem] when doing [type of task].

- Make your hypothesis as specific as possible. The narrower your focus, the faster your progress in proving it right or wrong.

- Create a target customer profile with your team using the traits continuum.

CHAPTER 3

Who Should I Be Talking To?

We went to Sonoma, the center of highbrow culinary thinking, and went to the Wine Auction. We bought a booth and had a KRAVE jerky tent next to the high-end wineries. There was definite shock factor! But people were intrigued and came to talk to us.

—Jon Sebastiani, CEO of KRAVE

Everyone wants to feel connected. When people know that they're actually helping to grow a product, that we want their personal experience to be as great as possible, it gets them really excited.

—Dan Levine, CTO of StyleSeat

There are probably two things concerning you right now: that you have no idea how to find the right customers to talk to, and that they wouldn't spend their time talking to you even if you could find them. If you have a product and existing customers, you may still find it surprisingly hard to get in direct contact with them. If you don't have a product yet, why would someone want to spend time talking to you about a product that doesn't even exist yet?

This chapter will tackle both of those fears head-on. You're going to learn how to use personal connections, social media, websites, and physical places to find the people who will benefit from the product you're trying to build. I'll also discuss the factors that motivate people to share and collaborate. By understanding some basic social psychology, you'll be better able to convince people to help you and make them feel happier for having done so. We'll cover:

- The importance of "earlyvangelists"
- Details for finding people to talk to
- Methods for interviews and preparations that ensure interviews run smoothly
- What to do if you can't find anyone who wants to talk

In effect, if you think of customer development interviews in terms of who, what, where, how, and when, this chapter helps you find out concretely who to talk to, decide how you will talk to them (in person, by telephone, or using video), where you'll do the interview (whether a physical place or the environment from which you'll conduct your phone or video interviews), and when (especially in terms of scheduling and spacing them). (Chapter 2 addressed the question of why you're doing the interviews to begin with.)

This chapter doesn't cover what questions you should ask interviewees. In fact, that's the wrong way to think of the *what* in customer development. The real what is what you should be learning from your interviews. We'll get there in Chapter 4.

By the end of this chapter, you'll be equipped to start reaching out to prospective customers immediately. The sooner you start sending out requests, the closer you'll be to validating your hypotheses.

How Can I Find Customers Before I've Even Built a Product?

This is one of the first questions people ask, and my response is always: *"How were you planning on finding them after you've built a product?"*

This isn't entirely meant as a snide answer—you'll be using many of the same techniques that you'd use once you have a product. Imagine a world where you weren't reading this book and you had just spent the past six months building your product. Now you're ready to sell it. What would you do?

- You'd look for relevant places to advertise.
- You'd seek out people likely to be interested in your product and give them pitches, demos, or samples.

- You'd look for places where your likely customers already are and try to get your product in front of them.

- You'd partner with complementary products or services to cross-promote.

- You'd build a website and monitor the channels bringing people to your site.

Every one of these methods can be started before you write a single line of code or sketch a single wireframe.

And by doing so, you can prevent having to add sad bullet points like these:

- You'd wonder if Google Analytics were broken because it's not showing any visitors to your site.

- You'd look at your garage filled with product and fear that you'll be reduced to dropping it off at Goodwill.

Come On—Why Would They Talk to Me?

Before we go into the details of techniques for finding customers, let's address the skepticism you're probably feeling. You may think, "So you're telling me that people are willing to spend time talking to someone they don't know who has no product to show them?"

I've found that no one believes this at face value. People are busy. They hate telemarketers, advertising, and spam. How is this different?

To start believing that people—useful people—will want to talk to you, you need to understand the people you're looking for.

The Importance of Earlyvangelists

In the beginning, you are looking for the most enthusiastic, passionate potential customers. These are the people who are the most motivated to solve their problem.

This doesn't mean you want "early adopters," those folks who always rush out to buy the latest device and pride themselves on tinkering with products or exploring all of the advanced features. Early adopters are willing to try just about anything! That won't help you validate or invalidate your hypotheses.

You need to find people who have the specific problem that you're trying to solve. They're often not early adopters, or particularly technologically savvy or eager to learn new things—they just need to solve their problem.

Another way of looking at this is that you're looking for the people who are suffering the most severe pain.

Steve Blank calls these people your "earlyvangelists"—people who are willing to take a risk on your unproven, unfinished product (Figure 3-1).

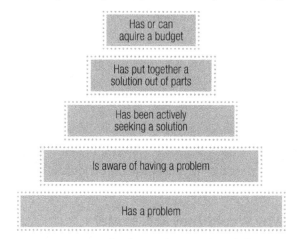

Figure 3-1. Steve Blank's earlyvangelist definition; in addition to having these characteristics, earlyvangelists share your vision*

Earlyvangelists will give you all the details about their problem, their needs, and their environment. They'll try your ugly, broken beta, send you unsolicited page-long emails full of bugs and suggestions, and then recommend you to everyone they know. This isn't something the earlyvangelist is doing as a favor to you. These customers have a problem that already has them excited or frustrated or angry. They see you and your potential product as something that might help alleviate that problem, so it's in their best interest to give you all the information you need to execute on a solution.

If you're reaching out to people who would consider it a burden to talk with you, you're approaching the wrong people. What you should be offering is a way for people to benefit their own self-interest by telling you what they know.

Three Things That Motivate People

Even after years of doing this, I'm always surprised by how many people respond to requests for their time. But then again, when I get requests for

---

* Source: *http://steveblank.com/2010/03/04/perfection-by-subtraction-the-minimum-feature-set/*

customer development interviews for other peoples' products, I genuinely look forward to them. Why is that?

Individuals are different, but human psychology is pretty universal. We're all motivated by the same desires:

- We like to help others
- We like to sound smart
- We like to fix things

Helping Others Makes Us Happy

How do these human tendencies help when you want talk with prospective customers about your idea?

You send out an email from your personal email address that addresses the recipient personally. The recipient sees it and says to himself: someone is asking for my help.

It's one of the few globally universal psychological constructs—regardless of culture or income, we derive happiness from investing our resources to help others.* Because you've specified *why* you want to talk with this specific person, the recipient has a feeling of ownership. He can't ignore it, assuming that someone else will deal with it.†

It seems that we particularly like giving our time to causes that align with our own self-identity.‡ So when you send an email asking someone to help you out by talking about something he's already interested in, that's a win-win.

We Like to Sound Smart

Your recipient responds and commits to a conversation with you. As you begin the conversation, you make it clear that she's the expert. You want to learn from her experiences.

Wanting to sound smart isn't as egotistical as it sounds; we are rewarded when we gain the respect of others. Psychologist Abraham Maslow defined

---

* *http://www.apa.org/pubs/journals/releases/psp-104-4-635.pdf*

† . The tendency to assume someone else will handle a problem is called "diffusion of responsibility." There's a similar effect, called "social loafing," where people in groups do less work than they would as an individual. I suspect the latter is responsible for the low response rates and lackluster answers that people give in surveys.

‡ When asked to volunteer, people prefer to give time over money to causes they are invested in. Furthermore, people experience greater happiness (and give more generously) when asked to donate time instead of money (see *http://www.escholarship.org/uc/item/8j02n364*).

this as esteem (achievement, respect of others, respect by others) and included it in his hierarchy of needs.* When I thank someone at the end of a customer development interview, it's common for him to reply with something like, "No, thank you! I'm so glad that I had something useful to share!"

My theory is that most of us are unrecognized experts in the things we do every day—whether it's keeping the family fed or debugging code or coordinating large meetings. It's a pleasant change to hear from someone who doesn't take that for granted.

Fixing Things Gives Us a Sense of Purpose

As your interviewee recounts his frustrations, he gets to vent and experience catharsis. But more importantly, as you ask follow-up questions, you give him the feeling that things can get better. That's not what we're used to:

> [W]e feel so helpless and hopeless about resolving our consumer complaints that a staggering 95% of consumer dissatisfactions go unresolved because we fail to complain effectively about them.... We are convinced that bringing up our complaints with the people responsible will be more trouble than it's worth, will not lead to a satisfying resolution and that it might actually make the situation worse. However, by pursuing a complaint successfully we can demonstrate our influence in our relationships and/or our social context and feel more capable, competent and empowered.†

Unless we personally experience the problems that we are trying to solve, it may still be difficult to imagine that customers will be eager to talk to us.

Come with me on a trip to the DMV

Think of a situation that is universally frustrating. In the United States, a trip to the Department of Motor Vehicles to renew your driver's license is the classic example.

Walk up to a group of people you don't know (say, in a coffee shop or at a bus stop). All you need to do is mention that you just took a trip to the DMV and the people around you will immediately start a conversation about it:

---

* http://en.wikipedia.org/wiki/Maslow%27s_hierarchy_of_needs

† http://www.psychologytoday.com/blog/the-squeaky-wheel/201101/how-attain-real-personal-empowerment

Oh man, last time I waited in line for hours and then when I got to the counter, the clerk told me I was missing a form!

You should book a DMV appointment online—last time I did that and I was in and out in 10 minutes!

I use the time to catch up on work-related reading so at least I get something productive done while I wait.

It's unlikely that you're waiting for a bus with unusually outspoken people, Department of Motor Vehicles employees, or advice columnists. The DMV is so universally awful that it elicits spontaneous help, expertise, and suggested improvements.

Yes, you're asking people to commit their time, and many people are short on time. But you're also offering them a positive opportunity to be helpful, sound smart, and make the world a better place, all in a 20-minute conversation.

How Can I Find My Customers?

Everyone who will potentially buy your product is out there somewhere. But unless this is a niche market that you're already deeply embedded in, it's tough to know where you'll find them. There are a variety of ways to find people, and it will probably take some trial and error to find the people who need your product.

Ask Your Connections for Introductions

Your first stop should be your immediate circle of friends and coworkers. (Presumably you're trying to enter a market that you and your connections know something about already; if your personal network is completely irrelevant, that's probably a sign that you're trying to enter a market you know nothing about, which is a terrible idea.)

How should you start? Just because you have 500 people in your contact list doesn't mean you should blast out an email with 500 recipients.

You don't have the time to interview a bunch of people who are obviously not relevant to the problem you're solving, and you don't have endless social capital to burn through.

It's not that you're going to ask your old boss, your child's soccer coach, and your Aunt Mabel for an interview (unless, of course, they have the problem that you are trying to solve). While you may already know some prospective customers, it's more likely that you'll find people within the larger universe of second-degree connections. You'll need to ask your connections to introduce you to their friends, coworkers, and family members who have the problem that you're trying to solve.

Would you introduce me to your friends who …?

A good rule of thumb is this: Anyone you ask for introductions should understand why you asked him specifically. When you ask your friend who does triathlons to connect you with amateur athletes, or your former coworker who works in the medical industry to connect you with nurses, the request will feel appropriate and a bit flattering.

Your friends and coworkers want to help you, but they're also wary. They're putting themselves on the line by vouching for you and putting their friends and colleagues into an unknown situation.

In order to unlock the networks of your friends and coworkers, you need to be very clear about what you are asking. You'll have to anticipate and address their biggest concerns: time, commitment, privacy, and content. You'll also need to make it as easy and painless as possible for them to connect you with relevant people they know.

The lowest-friction approach is to describe the type of people you need to talk with and convince friends to give you contact information so that you can reach out directly. It rarely works, though. Your friends are unlikely to feel comfortable unless they remain the intermediary. If they forward on an email, it also makes it clearer that they're vouching for you. This helps with response rate and setting your interviewees' minds at ease.*

Asking for Introductions

Here's the information that your message to friends and colleagues should include. I always send these requests via email, even if I've just been on a phone call or had a face-to-face conversation with the person.

Don't try to save time by sending a mass email. An individually crafted message is asking a personal favor; a generic email with recipients in the Bcc: header is an easily ignorable spam.

---

* It can also keep your message from landing in the recipient's spam folder.

You're crafting this message to make it as easy as possible for your connection to help you. She may choose to simply forward your message, edit it as she wishes, or summarize it via another medium:

- Briefly (5–10 words) state the type of problem you're working on

- Acknowledge why you believe your connection can help

- Ask if she is willing to forward a message to relevant people she knows

- Acknowledge how helpful this contact will be

- Explicitly ask for her to forward your message

- Include a ready-to-forward prewritten message that explains what you're looking for, the amount of time commitment, and an assurance of privacy

Here's what your message might look like:

I'm trying to learn more about how engineering teams are embracing more agile methodologies. As a recruiter, I know you have a ton of connections with engineering hiring managers! Can you help me out by forwarding this message to a few relevant folks?

For people who respond, I'll be reaching out to set up a **20-minute phone call** to ask about their current engineering process.

It won't be something that requires advance preparation; just hearing about their experiences would be a huge help for the project I'm working on. I've included a message below that you can forward:

- - -

My name is _____, and I want to learn more about how engineering teams are experimenting with agile development methodologies for a project I'm working on.

It would be incredibly helpful for me to hear about your experiences and ask you a few questions. It won't take more than 20 minutes, and there's no need to prepare in advance.

Can I schedule a call with you for sometime next week?

Thanks,

[include your name and contact information]

_____

Casting a Wider Net

For many of you, personal connections and direct introductions are not going to lead to enough relevant people. Most likely, you'll need to try a variety of approaches to figure out what works.

Finding people on LinkedIn

LinkedIn is typically the easiest way to find people who work in a specific industry or hold a certain job title. LinkedIn also allows you to narrow your search based on skills and expertise.* (Of course, job title and experience are usually more relevant for enterprise products than for consumer products.)

You can probably find at least a couple of people who fit your criteria and are first- or second-degree connections. That may be all you need to seed your initial search: one or two receptive people can help you identify more people you should be talking to.

You can send messages directly to your first-degree connections, either through LinkedIn's own messaging system or by finding the person's contact email address on their profile. (You'll need to be logged in to LinkedIn to see her full profile.) If someone is a second-degree connection, LinkedIn allows you to ask the common contact to forward a message to him (Figure 3-2).

Figure 3-2. When sending messages to a second-degree connection, include a ready-to-forward snippet to make the introduction easier for your contact

* For more tactical how-to advice for using LinkedIn, check out this great blog post from Mark Horoszowski, CEO of MovingWorlds: *http://customerdevlabs.com/2012/06/24/anybody-that-knocks-linkedin-does-not-know-how-to-use-it/*.

I don't recommend forwarding messages to a third-degree LinkedIn connection. With two degrees of separation, the sense of being vouched for fades a lot. If you want to reach out to third-degree connections and maximize your odds of getting a response, you're better off upgrading to a premium subscription and using LinkedIn inMail to directly contact people.

LinkedIn includes inMail credits with premium subscriptions. Because it costs money to send these messages, the recipients are somewhat less likely to perceive them as spam. Your inMails only count against your total if the recipient accepts your message—so you can do some tweaking of your message cheaply. A premium subscription gives you access to additional filters, which can also help you find people.

In some cases, searching LinkedIn serves as a lightweight customer development tool. You may find that your advanced search for a specific job title and industry combination doesn't return as many results as you expected—in other words, your target market may be too small.

One of the challenges with LinkedIn is that you are competing with recruiters, some of whom take a spray-and-pray approach to any person who meets some vague keyword searches. How do you differentiate yourself? Be specific, be personalized, and be brief.

Introducing Yourself via LinkedIn

LinkedIn messages have a 1,000-character limit, so you'll need to be brief in describing your purpose and method. Here's the information to include:

- Acknowledge why this person specifically can help you

- Briefly (5–10 words) state the type of problem you're working on

- Clearly state a minimal request for time (e.g., a three-question survey or a five-minute call)

Your message may look something like this:

Hi, my name is _____, and I'm trying to learn more about how small companies choose SaaS products. Can you take two minutes to answer this three-question survey? [URL]

I appreciate your time, and I'm happy to return the favor however I can!

Thanks,

_____

Surveys are not intended to replace customer interviews. In this scenario, the survey serves two purposes. It allows you to ask a couple of screening questions to ensure that this is a relevant target customer, and more importantly, it serves as a foot in the door to make initial contact. Because contacting people via LinkedIn is somewhat impersonal, you'll need to make your initial request as lightweight as possible in order to get responses. Once you've started a conversation with someone, she's far more likely to agree to follow-up questions or a longer interview.

Finding people on Quora

Quora works well as a tool for finding people for both consumer and enterprise products, though the site remains somewhat skewed toward technology topics and the Internet-savvy. (Quora initially launched by invitation only; the early community was heavily concentrated among San Francisco and New York technical circles.)

Quora has a much smaller user base than LinkedIn or Twitter, but tends to attract more passionate and vocal people. I've typically had better luck connecting with people via Quora, and I suspect this is why. (I've also noticed that I'm personally more likely to respond to messages sent to my Quora inbox than to my LinkedIn inbox.)

If you use Quora, you'll want to do some homework first. Quora users are fairly protective of their community. Be a contributing member, not just a taker. Cover the basics: upload a photo, complete your profile information, and follow relevant topics. Spend some time reading questions and answers in the topics relevant to your product area. Try to write some answers, or at least comment on some answers, in a way that adds value to the community *without* self-promotion.

As a bonus, going through that exercise will probably give you ideas for additional questions to ask. People who have written questions or comments on the topics you're following are a good place to start. They've self-identified as experts who are probably willing to continue talking on the topic. But even the people who have followed the question have demonstrated some intent and may be receptive to your messages (Figure 3-3).

Please do not solicit customer development participants in a Quora thread. Your question will be down-voted swiftly and annoy the very people that you're hoping to learn from.

Instead, you'll want to craft individual private messages for each person. When you find an interesting person, click on her name to get to her profile page. From a user's profile page, there is a link to send her a direct message in the sidebar. (It's somewhat hidden; see Figure 3-4.)

Question Stats

Latest activity 4 Oct, 2012

This question has **1** monitor with **426631** topic followers.

448 views on this question.

13 people are following this question.

Figure 3-3. People following the Quora question "Customer Development: How did you test and run a hypothesis?"

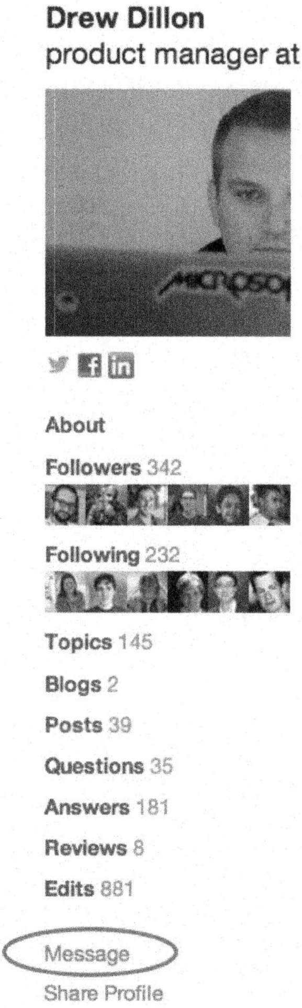

Drew Dillon
product manager at

About

Followers 342

Following 232

Topics 145

Blogs 2

Posts 39

Questions 35

Answers 181

Reviews 8

Edits 881

Message

Share Profile

Figure 3-4. In the lefthand sidebar of a user's profile page, you can use the Message link to send him a private message

Start by sending only a couple of outreach messages to Quora users and then wait to make sure that your message was effective. (You don't want to burn through all of your prospects if your message needs tweaking.) You may need to wait a couple of days to receive a response if people have turned off the notification that emails them when they have a new private message.

Finding people on forums and private online communities

Looking for parents, BMW enthusiasts, chronic disease survivors, dieters, or wine connoisseurs? You're less likely to find them on a general-interest community site like Quora than on a topic-specific forum, mailing list, or membership-based community.

Many of these communities are publicly discoverable, but the most effective way of finding the best ones is to ask a target customer: "If you wanted to find the best recommendations for [topic], where would you go?"

Don't treat these communities as only a place for harvesting customer development interviewees—respect the established culture and community. Just reading through the conversations gives you a lightweight method for validating ideas—you'll see which topics attract dozens of responses and which go unanswered. This is a good proxy for what pains and what motivates your potential customers!

As with Quora, it's important to start by contributing to the community. Lurk and read the conversations for a while, then provide some answers (factual answers are safer than opinions). Use your participation as a way to connect with a few individuals rather than broadcasting a request for interviews.

Finding people in the offline world

Sometimes the simplest way to find your prospective customers is to physically go where they are. You'll never find more runners congregated than at the end of a 5K or half-marathon; you'll never find more dental professionals than at the Starbucks across the street from a major dentistry conference.

Intercepting people in the real world can be more sensitive because you'll have to interrupt them. The trick is to think through the tasks that your prospective customer needs to complete (getting in line, networking with a potential business partner, getting that cute girl's number, completing his purchase)—and don't approach until *after* those tasks are complete.

You're also more likely to have time constraints (the runner is probably too sweaty and thirsty to talk for long; the dentist probably needs to hurry back so he doesn't miss the next session). Don't plan on a full interview. Focus on a single question, or quickly pitch the problem and ask for contact information so that you can follow up later.

Conferences offer sponsorship opportunities, but if you've ever worked a conference booth you know that depressingly few people come over to talk to you (unless you're bribing them with really appealing tchotchkes or raffle prizes). You'll need to actively approach people to get them to answer questions or share contact information.

Go Where Your Prospective Customers Already Are

Beef jerky alongside fine wine?

"There was a perception of beef jerky as a low-value snack, as male-dominated junk food that you'd purchase at a gas station," says Jon Sebastiani, CEO of KRAVE. But Sebastiani saw the trend toward high-protein diets and organic foods and hypothesized that consumers were ready for a gourmet option. He wondered, "Is it too much of a challenge to change the perception of the entire category? That was our original question."

Sebastiani started in Sonoma, which he jokingly calls "the center of highbrow culinary thinking, where people are almost outright arrogant about their food choices." He went where his prospective customers already were: the local Whole Foods and the annual Wine Auction event.

At the same time, Sebastiani was enrolled in Steve Blank's Lean LaunchPad course in the Berkeley-Columbia executive MBA program.* Each week, he brought what he'd learned into class and got feedback from Blank.

---

* I was a participating mentor in Steve's class, so I got to hear KRAVE's progress week by week. Before the course was over, I was able to buy KRAVE jerky from my neighborhood Safeway, which was pretty amazing.

The KRAVE team was surprised by how enthusiastically potential customers validated their hypothesis. "It was as though we'd unlocked this pent-up demand for quality jerky. People secretly loved jerky and they wanted to know where they could buy the good stuff."

Having validated customer demand for a high-end jerky, KRAVE needed to make sure that its product could meet those expectations. Sebastiani asked potential customers how they made buying decisions, what nutritional information they looked at, and how they defined natural, healthy snack products. Nitrates and artificial ingredients were out. "We were shocked by how far we had to go, nutritionally, to be considered a premium product," says Sebastiani.

Of course, customer demand is only half of the equation. To reach its target customers, KRAVE needed to be available on store shelves. For distributors and retailers, new products are a risk. "There's so much competition for shelf space. Every square inch costs them money. They make decisions based on consumer trends—they have to believe that the customer is going to spend money on this product." Sebastiani was able to bring the output of his customer interviews to Safeway, which won him his first $500,000 product order.* "We were able to prove that the customer was ready," says Sebastiani. He used sales data from Safeway to help him win his next supermarket pitch.

KRAVE is now carried in over 15,000 stories in the United States and Canada and sold over $12 million of product in 2012. But don't look for it next to the Slim Jims—you'll find KRAVE Basil Citrus or Sweet Chipotle jerky next to Clif Bars, Odwalla, PopChips, and other offerings in the health food aisles.

---

* *http://www.nytimes.com/2013/02/17/business/krave-jerky-seeks-to-upgrade-a-snacks-image.html*

Using blog posts

There may not be very many people who care enough to author an entire blog on the area you're exploring, but the ones that do exist are definitely written by people you need to connect with! A few of the more comprehensive blog aggregators are:

- Alltop.com

- Blogarama.com

- Blogs.com

Of course, there are far fewer blogs entirely devoted to a particular topic than there are individual blog posts on a topic. For finding standalone blog posts on a specific topic, you don't need a blog aggregator; you need a search engine.

Trial-and-error searches, patience, and a lot of open browser tab windows will eventually yield results. One tip: if you're using Google Search, click on the Search Tools button and change the "Any time" option to "Past year" (Figure 3-5). You need to find people who experienced your problem recently, not back in 2005.

| Web | Images | Maps | Shopping | News | More ▾ | Search tools |

| Past year ▾ | Sorted by relevance ▾ | All results ▾ | Clear |

Any time	ɟp ⓘ
Past hour	Course - **startup**validation.co
	:o/
Past 24 hours	dea before investing time and money!
Past week	
	ipedia, the free encyclopedia
Past month	an_Startup
✓ Past year	:artup" is an approach for launching businesses and products,
	earning, scientific experimentation, and iterative product
Custom range...	n - Definitions - The Lean Startup book

Figure 3-5. Use Google's "Past year" filter to omit out-dated search results when hunting for blog posts

Using Twitter

Twitter is one of the harder ways to connect directly with people due to the lack of public contact information. You can @mention a specific person, but then you have less than 140 characters in which to make a request or introduce yourself. Twitter is often more useful for people or companies who already have a following. Because you have an existing relationship with your followers, you can post a simple request with a link to a survey and use that to collect contact information.

For the majority of people, the most productive use of Twitter is simply to find the relevant hashtags that your target customer uses or to read the articles that she is sharing. For example, product managers often add #prodmgmt to their tweets; parents of autistic children may tag their tweets with #autism. Searching for one of those hashtags is a good way to find the articles that your target population is interested in, as well as offline locations such as conferences or events where they may be physically present.

No matter what type of customer you're targeting, you can ask yourself what they are already doing. What products or services are they already buying? What websites are they already using? Where do they spend their time? When they have a large purchase to make, how do they research it and who do they ask for advice?

Not using Craigslist

I'm going to save you the time of writing a post and being flagged: don't use Craigslist to directly find people to talk to. There are a huge number of scams posted every day, and your request for a conversation is going to look just as suspicious. The people you need to talk to are not scanning the gig offerings looking for interview opportunities. Offering paid compensation only lures the desperate and unemployed.

But it is possible that your target customer is transacting on Craigslist already. Is the problem you're looking to solve related to real estate, dating, job hunting or posting, or local events? If so, your target customer may already be scouring Craigslist.

For many people, this type of contact may be crossing a line. The guy looking for a dog-friendly apartment may be exactly the type of person you want to talk to, but you're being deceptive in emailing him (unless you happen to have a line on a great one-bedroom across the street from a dog park). If you choose this path, be judicious and be ready for accusations of spam.

To Pay or Not to Pay?

"How much should I pay the people I interview?"

My default answer: Nothing.

Don't interpret this to mean that you're taking advantage of people or devaluing their time. Quite the opposite. You are compensating your interviewees by giving them your time, attention, and attempts to solve a problem that is causing them pain.

You are practicing customer development because you need to validate that people who take this particular problem seriously do in fact exist. Before you invest time and money developing a solution, you need a high degree of confidence that you'll have buyers. If someone is not willing to invest in a 20-minute conversation without a monetary incentive, what are the odds that she'll write you a check in six months?

This doesn't mean, of course, that you should be a one-sided taker. While you are hoping to learn certain things, you must allow the conversation to develop in accordance with what your customer wants to talk about. It's highly personal, and that is a more valuable form of compensation. When talking with existing customers, you are implicitly offering some of your own time in the future.

This isn't to say that you should never spend a cent on prospective customers. If you're trying to find participants at Starbucks, you should buy them coffee. If you're asking for someone's extracurricular time, you may want to offer a tangible thank you of some kind. (At Yammer, we offer customers the choice of where to direct a small charitable contribution. It's just enough to make people feel like they did a second good deed for the day.) That's the point—what you offer should feel more like an appreciation of their time than *payment* for it.

Using a landing page

Building a landing page and using Google AdWords to direct traffic to it was the original customer development tactic. Eric Ries wrote about it and many companies (including KISSmetrics) used that method. But as more businesses have begun using AdWords, the price per click has gotten much more expensive. The cost of acquiring visitors via AdWords may be prohibitively high unless you are in a narrow niche.

However, if you have a large Twitter following, a popular blog, or a base of existing customers, you can get a reasonable amount of site traffic. You can build it yourself or use a hosted service like LaunchRock (*http://www.launchrock.com*), which also helps you promote the site via Twitter. The advantage of using a landing page is that it's easy to combine a short survey with the ability to follow up and contact people for a longer interview (Figure 3-6).

1. When was the last time you rented a car?

○ In the past week

○ In the past month

○ In the past 3 months

○ In the past year

○ More than a year ago

2. How many airplane flights have you taken in the past year?

[   ]

3. Can you help me out by participating in a 15-minute phone interview? I'd like to learn more about how people travel and would love to hear from you!

○ No

○ Yes, my contact email address is: [   ] *

Figure 3-6. A short survey helps qualify potential customers without hurting your response rate; be sure to collect email addresses so you can follow up*

How Should I Conduct My Interviews?

The best method for conducting customer development interviews is the one that is most convenient for you and your target customers. There are pros and cons to each approach, but those don't matter if it takes too long to coordinate schedules or if you find yourself postponing or rescheduling interviews. I'll walk through a few methods and explain why they may or may not work for you.

Visiting the Customer's Home or Office

Intuit calls visiting the customer's home or office "Follow Me Home"; user researchers may refer to this as an ethnographic interview or a field visit. This method predates the lean startup movement by decades.†

---

*   It is possible to create a standalone survey without a landing page, using a free tool like SurveyMonkey or Wufoo (I prefer Wufoo). The downside of a standalone survey is that it has less credibility than a landing page—which leads to lower response rates.

†   Literally, decades! Intuit pioneered the "Follow Me Home" program in 1989. "[The program] called for an Intuit employee to hang around the local computer store until someone bought Quicken off the shelf (this was back when people did that sort of thing). The employee would then ask the buyer to take him home so he could see how difficult the product was to install. He would watch the process silently, noting everything from how easily the shrinkwrap came off to which lines of direction bred that confused look on the new user's face" (*http://www.inc. com/magazine/20040401/25cook.html*).

Observing the customer in his natural environment is the highest-fidelity method of customer development. You'll learn about factors like noise level, neatness of the environment, whether your customer has privacy or is constantly interrupted, whether he has outdated or upgraded technology, and who comes to talk to him while you're there. If you ask a question about how the customer does something, he can show you, not just describe it.

Face-to-face conversations are more personal; he can see your face and body language, which helps in building a relationship with this potential earlyvangelist. You may also meet other people in the household or workplace for later follow-up questions.

On-site interviews are by far the hardest to coordinate. Privacy concerns may prevent employees from bringing an outsider into their office, or at least require getting an NDA signed in advance. For consumers, a messy home or distractions from family members may discourage the customer from agreeing to talk. The need to obtain permission or approval in advance may also lead to delays or last-minute cancellations.

On-site interviews work well for:

- Companies with existing products and customers (more about this in Chapter 8)

- Problems where the physical environment plays a role

- Problems that involve multiple stakeholders

- Products used in the home

In-Person Conversations in a Neutral Location

Another high-fidelity method for customer development interviews is a face-to-face conversation in a neutral public location. Even if you don't know what the prospective customer's noisy cubicle or messy kitchen looks like, you can see his body language and watch his facial expressions as he describes his problem situations. Because he can see you as well, this method helps build rapport with the customer.

The cons are similar to those with the site visit. You'll need to identify appropriate venues. Once you've found them, your customer has to figure out how to get there, park her car, and (assuming you've never met before) figure out how to identify you. I find this method to be the most challenging for note-taking (there is often background noise, and sometimes a lack of reliable surfaces to write on).

In-person interviews at a neutral location work well for:

- Interviews where you wish to speak with two or more people together, but want to avoid having any of them be distracted by family members or coworkers (such as spouses or business partners)
- Consumer products where the audience is general enough that you can try to string together back-to-back interviews in a Starbucks or another public place

Phone Conversations

This is the method that I most commonly use for customer development interviews.

I don't get any visual information, but I can learn a lot from verbal intonations and pauses. (I also suspect that people may be more honest about things that embarrass or frustrate them when they don't have to make eye contact.)

More importantly, I can conduct interviews faster so I can learn faster. When I ask for phone conversations, I get higher response rates. Scheduling is easier because no one has to account for travel time or other people's permission. I can take more comprehensive notes because I can type on my laptop without appearing rude.

Phone interviews work well for:

- Connecting with busy people
- Talking with customers in different locations and time zones
- Completing as many interviews as possible in a short period of time

Video Chat or Call with Screen Sharing

Video chats share most of the same advantages and disadvantages as phone conversations. You also gain the benefit of seeing the customer's facial expressions and body language and potentially even what's on her computer screen. If your target customer is tech-savvy (or younger than 20), this is a great option. If not, approach with caution. After spending 5 minutes trying to figure out if video is working, your flustered customer is not going to be able to give you the best possible information in the remaining 15 minutes.

Video chats work well for:

- Tech-savvy audiences comfortable with setting up video conferencing
- Interviews where seeing the user's computer screen is critical for understanding his usage or frustrations

Instant Messaging

I'll admit it: instant messaging (IM) is not my favorite approach for conducting interviews. Text-only communication provides the least amount of information with the highest risk of misinterpretation. Most of us have difficulty interpreting the intent or emotional severity of written messages.* I've also noticed through various user research projects over the years that people are more self-conscious and more likely to self-censor what they *write* than what they *say*.

Still, sometimes text-based communication is the best available option. Live chat apps give you the opportunity to have a conversation with someone while he's on your site. If you don't talk with that prospective customer in real time, you'll have no way to contact him in the future. You also may want to schedule conversations over IM if you're concerned about audio quality—talking with interviewees in other countries when voice-over-IP is unreliable or talking with interviewees whose accents make it difficult to understand what they're saying.

IM works well for:

- Prospective customers who are less comfortable speaking verbally (people who are shy, have thick accents, or want to control the information they share)

- Conversations where it's important to exchange data such as URLs or snippets of code

Following Up

You've probably noticed that the templates for an initial introduction message haven't included scheduling. You need to keep the initial message short if you don't know the recipient personally.

Scheduling adds two or more sentences that weigh down your message. Messages that are too long don't get responses; they are mentally set aside until we have time to read them (which is never).

---

* Asked to determine whether a message was serious or sarcastic, only 56% of people correctly identified the tone of an email (versus over 75% for verbal recordings). "Email is fine if you just want to communicate content, but not any emotional material." For more information, see *http://www.apa.org/monitor/feb06/egos.aspx*. As you'll learn in Chapter 4, emotions are extremely important to prioritizing information, so I do not recommend this method overall.

Are Your Messages Mobile-Friendly?

Keep in mind that your recipient is increasingly likely to be reading your message on his phone. Litmus states that 51% of emails were opened on mobile phones as of December 2013.*

Try sending yourself a copy of the email first and viewing it on your phone (see Figure 3-7). Would someone have to scroll just to get to the point? If so, aim to cut your message length in half.

---

* https://litmus.com/blog/mobile-opens-hit-51-percent-android-claims-number-3-spot

Figure 3-7. Here's a too-long email on my phone; the meat of the message—what you want me to do, when you want to talk—is buried unless I scroll down

Scheduling Phone Interviews

Once you've gotten an affirmative response from a person, then you can go into more tactical detail. Your job: to make it incredibly easy for her to commit to a time to talk.

Thank you for your willingness to help me out!

I'd like to schedule a 20-minute call so I can learn from you. You don't need to prepare in advance; just hearing about your experiences with _____, from your personal perspective, will be a huge help to me.

Does one of these times work for you?

Monday, July 8 9am PST (12pm EST)

Monday, July 8 11:30am PST (2:30pm EST)

Tuesday, July 9 7am PST (10am EST)

Thursday, July 11 2pm PST (5pm EST)

For a phone call, I recommend offering three or four options, not all on the same day of the week or the same hour of the day. Make sure you are explicit about what time zone you are proposing.

Better yet, figure out in advance if your interviewee lives in a different time zone and suggest appropriate times. A 9 a.m. call isn't a considerate suggestion if you are in New York and your interviewee is in Los Angeles.

If you use Gmail, I recommend downloading a browser plug-in called Rapportive (*http://www.rapportive.com*). When you type in an email address, Rapportive pulls associated publicly available data from LinkedIn, Twitter, and Google and displays it in a sidebar next to your message compose window. It may include a photo, a location, a job title, and recent social media posts (Figure 3-8).

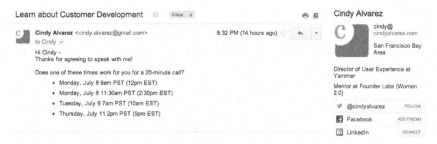

Figure 3-8. Rapportive shows you a sidebar with information the person has shared on social media: avatar, location, job title

If you use Outlook on Windows, you can use the Outlook Social Connector (*http://www.linkedin.com/static?key=microsoft_outlook*) to view relevant LinkedIn information as you're composing a message. Not all consumers have LinkedIn profiles, but most businesspeople or information workers have a profile that contains at least location and job title.

Scheduling Face-to-Face Interviews

The best locations for face-to-face interviews are convenient for both cars and public transit, have plenty of space, and don't suffer from so much popularity that you won't be able to find a table or quiet area. I usually suggest meeting at Starbucks; they're accustomed to people having work meetings and their WiFi is reliable. Hotels with large, quiet lobbies are also a good option.

Here's an example I used at KISSmetrics:

> *Thanks for signing up for the KISSmetrics beta list. I'd love to get a half-hour of your time to talk over coffee. Does one of these sugges-tions work for you?*
>
> > *9:30 a.m. on Tues, May 10 at Greenhouse Cafe in West Portal*
> >
> > *3 p.m. on Thurs, May 12 at Farley's Coffeehouse in Potrero Hill*
> >
> > *11:30 a.m. on Fri, May 13 at Starbucks near the Metreon*
>
> *Feel free to suggest another time if none of these work for you—I can make it anywhere within San Francisco between 9 a.m.–4 p.m.*
>
> *Thanks!*
>
> *Cindy*

This gives the recipient all of the necessary information she needs to make a decision: expected time outlay, times she can check against her calendar, information about the venue,* and locations (so she doesn't schedule back-to-back meetings at opposite ends of town).

Odds are that sending a message with several options will eliminate the need for playing email tag to schedule a meeting. But even if the interviewee can't accept one of your suggestions, you've set some parameters so that she can easily propose an alternative that is likely to work.

---

* I typically include links to Yelp in the email—that gives your interviewee easy access to the venue's name and address plus a map, which makes it easy for her to retrieve step-by-step directions if she has a smartphone.

Once the interviewee has chosen a time, I recommend sending a calendar invitation as well as your cell phone number. It's also useful to send a reminder email the day before, or in the morning before an afternoon call.

Spacing Your Interviews

Most of you won't find yourself trying to cram in interviews from the dozens of prospective customers who immediately agree to talk to you. (If you do, congratulations! That's a good problem to have.) But you may think that you'll set aside a half-day and try to cram in as many interviews as possible in that time period. In the beginning, that's not setting yourself up for success.

You need time to prepare, time to do the interview, and time to go over your notes right after the interview and let the most important things surface. Then you need a few minutes to prepare for the next interview. (The amount of time you'll need between interviews falls dramatically after you've gained some comfort in conducting them, but in the beginning you'll need the breaks.)

For this reason, I suggest that you start by scheduling no more than one 20–30 minute interview per hour (Figure 3-9).

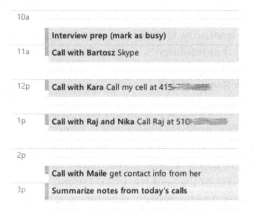

Figure 3-9. Your interview schedule may look like this; you should block off time before an appointment for prep and some time afterward for summarizing notes, which I'll talk about more in Chapter 6

Why would you do that?

- To make sure you really get 30 minutes to talk if the interview starts a few minutes late

- To make sure that if the conversation is really going strong, you can let your interviewee keep talking for up to 45 minutes (in Chapter 5 I'll tell you why I think interviews longer than that reach a point of diminishing returns)

- To give yourself time immediately afterward to go over your notes and get a fix on the most important things you learned

- To give yourself a quick break before the next interview

Over time you'll be able to schedule interviews closer together. I'm usually comfortable scheduling two 20-minute interviews in the same hour. Now that I have more expertise interviewing, I can typically maximize the information I get from the interviewee in the first 20 minutes. It's also gotten easier for me to context-switch from one call to the next. It will get easier for you the more interviews you do!

Interview Troubleshooting

In my experience, you'll be surprised by how often things go well. Since you'll have some questions if you're new to customer development interviews, let's cover what might go wrong and how to deal with it.

What If No One Responds?

After you send an initial request to talk, I recommend waiting at least a few days to respond. For business customers, I typically wait a week. At that point, I'll resend the request with an additional message like "I'd still love to talk with you. If you're available this week, let me know and I can coordinate a time." About 20% of the time, the interviewee responds to this follow-up email and we successfully schedule and complete an interview. If you don't hear back, I don't recommend pursuing the person further. Don't be annoying.

If you've sent out a number of requests and no one has responded, conscript a friend or colleague to read your message and give you feedback. Making your message shorter or clearer, or changing the tone may be all you need.

What if you've gotten feedback on your message, improved it, and then sent 10 or more requests that still haven't netted any responses? Well, consider that your first hypothesis invalidation. Either you're reaching out to the wrong people or the topic you've mentioned isn't interesting. If this happens, you may want to return to Chapter 2 and revise your hypothesis.

Interview No-Shows

In my experience, somewhere between 5% to 10% of the interviews you schedule will end up in cancelations or no-shows.

When I did usability testing and scheduled sessions all day long, I actually planned my day around this. My rule of thumb was that 1 out of 10 participants would be a no-show. Because of this, I'd typically schedule sessions without a break. (This meant that when I did get a full turnout I had to skip lunch.)

In my experience, customer development tends to have a lower rate of no-shows than usability testing. I think this is because customer development takes a personal approach to recruiting participants; it's harder to disappoint a known individual than a faceless user research recruiter.

If an interviewee cancels or fails to show up, wait a day or two and then send a message offering to reschedule. Typically the interviewee responds and you'll be able to reschedule successfully, but if you don't get a response, let it go.

Next Step: Get Ready for Customer Development Interviews

Now you've got the tools to get in contact with your target customers, wherever they may be. You probably won't need to use all the methods described in this chapter. Once you've tried a few, it will be clear which methods are most successful in helping you reach the first few people (who will, in turn, lead you to more potential interviewees). The next chapter discusses what you'll be learning from these target customers and what questions to ask to elicit the most valuable and actionable insights.

Key Takeaways

- Find the people whose problem is most severe; they are eager to solve it and may become earlyvangelists.

- People will talk to you because we all like to help others, like to sound smart, like to fix things, and like to complain.

- Ask connections to introduce you to their friends. Explain why you're asking them in particular.

- Find people online using LinkedIn, Quora, Twitter, discussion groups, forums—but not Craigslist.

- Find people offline by going where your target customers hang out.

- In your initial reach-out message, be clear and brief, and make it easy for interviewees to respond.

- Leave time between interviews in case conversations go long and so you can review notes before the next interview.

CHAPTER 4

What Should I Be Learning?

The hard part about figuring out what customers want is figuring out that you need to figure it out.

—Paul Graham, Founder and Partner of Y Combinator

Spend time understanding all aspects of the customer value proposition. Ask yourself: why should your customer buy your product? How does your product fit into the rest of his world? What influences his opinion of the product's value? What is your product displacing—all products displace something—and why your customer should risk making that switch?

—Gary Swart, CEO of oDesk

When I first started doing customer development interviews, I spent hours coming up with a long list of perfect questions that were specific to my audience and product. I wrote down far more questions than I thought I could cover in a 30-minute interview in order to be prepared for any direction the conversation might take.

It didn't take long to realize that the pages of notes from a single interview came from the first few *basic* questions.

After all, your biggest risk comes from one of two common errors: that you failed to solve a problem that your customer has, or that you failed to make the solution attractive enough for your customer to choose it.

This chapter starts with the basic questions that I use in almost every interview. These work across a variety of customer and industry types.

We'll also cover:

- Why customers don't know what they want

- What you should be listening and prompting for

- Getting subjective answers from objective questions

The second half of this chapter delves into social psychology, but it's not purely theoretical: understanding how people think will help you ask effective questions. We'll talk about how to overcome people's natural limitations and biases (including your own).

Get Started with These Customer Development Questions

I don't vary my interview script much at all from project to project or company to company. I might add one completely custom question or adapt my tone to fit my audience, but otherwise I follow the same basic script.

Basic Customer Development Questions

- Tell me about how you do _____ today....

- Do you use any [tools/products/apps/tricks] to help you get _____ done?

- If you could wave a magic wand and be able to do anything that you can't do today, what would it be? Don't worry about whether it's possible, just anything.

- Last time you did _____, what were you doing right before you got started? Once you finished, what did you do afterward?

- Is there anything else about _____ that I should have asked?

If you're taking notes on a laptop, you can save a template document with about eight blank lines after each question and take notes directly into that.

Don't worry about a more structured form for taking notes; just get down as much detail as possible.

You may be wondering how just five questions can take up a 20-minute interview. These are not the only questions I ask, but they are the only *scripted* questions I ask. (See the Appendix to learn more about different types of questions and what you can expect to learn from them.)

As the customer talks, I'll respond with open-ended questions that are triggered by what she just said. Depending on the conversation, these might be things like:

- Can you tell me more about how that process goes?
- Who is involved in making that decision?
- Last time you did _____, how long did it take?
- Where did you most recently go to buy _____?
- May I ask, why did you come to that conclusion?

Think of these as conversational prompts more than questions. You can use them to keep the customer talking or to redirect him to a slightly different topic. If you're too busy writing notes to ask these prompt questions, that's a good problem to have. The customer is talking!

Customers Don't Know What They Want!

"It's not the customer's job to know what they want." —Steve Jobs

How is it that customers so often don't seem to know what they want? There's an obvious tension between customer wants and needs. You may be skeptical that customers can reveal things that product builders (who spend their days immersed in a technology, an industry, a business model) don't already know.

"Our customers just don't have good ideas." I've heard that on more than one occasion, and I'd be lying if I told you that I don't agree.

Most of us have had the maddening experience of building something based on customer feedback, only to find that the customer still isn't happy (or didn't buy the product after all). After this happens a few times, many companies conclude that customers are difficult, flaky, or don't know what they're talking about. Voice-of-the-customer feedback becomes something to dutifully collect and then mostly ignore.

Given the fact that this book has the word "customer" in the title, I think you can guess how vehemently I feel about that. *Don't ignore what your customers say.*

But it's worth taking some time to dig into exactly *why* customers are unreliable at telling us what they want and what they'll buy. And I'm going to start using the word "we" in talking about this—because you and I are subject to these same limitations.

No one knows better than your customer what it's like to live in his world. But that doesn't mean that he will be able to automatically put his experiences into words.

Customers know which cultural, time, and resource constraints affect them, but they don't mention them unprompted.

Once we get used to limitations, we stop questioning or even noticing them. It doesn't occur to us to mention constraints if we think of them as just the way things are. Sociologists call these taken-for-granted assumptions.

Customers know what they've tried in the past that hasn't worked, but they won't remember to tell you about it.

Our brains are biased toward things that have happened recently. We don't tend to mention past failures when we're proposing new solutions. If we've abandoned a process or tool, we may not immediately remember what parts of that solution *did* work.

Customers are (at least somewhat) aware of their capabilities and limitations, but probably won't volunteer them.

They know the methods they feel comfortable with and where they have good intentions but terrible follow-through. We often don't volunteer that we are bad at certain skills or processes.

Customers are proficient in the tools and processes they use, but it doesn't mean they understand how they work.

Proficiency does not require understanding how a tool or process works. "Any sufficiently advanced technology is indistinguishable from magic," writes science fiction author Arthur C. Clarke, and that isn't far from how most people view the products they use every day. The fact that I can ask my iPhone a question and get a reasonable answer certainly feels like magic to me. As the people who build products, we're immersed in our worlds. We're familiar with what technology and process and automation can do. Our customers may be 10 years behind us.

The customer is the expert, but that doesn't mean you can sit back and listen to what he has to say. Instead, you will have to direct him to push beyond surface-level answers.

You need to guide the conversation and set expectations, but also defer to the customer's experience. To overcome this tension, you'll be asking questions that have no clear right or wrong answer. You'll state your questions as objectively as possible and prompt the customer for personal and subjective responses.

Customers may not know what they want, but they can't hide what they need.

It's your job to uncover those needs. It's your job to get the details so that you can deduce why or how the previous solutions didn't work. It's your job to make him feel comfortable enough to be honest about those things with you.

The Problem Isn't What You Think It Is

What is a milkshake?

To think of a milkshake as the combination of ice cream, milk, and artificial flavorings is to think in terms of the *solution*. It doesn't tell you anything about the *problem* that the customer is trying to solve.

As people who build products, we think about them from the perspective of the benefits that we're creating. We want to be the best in our category. If we are trying to sell milkshakes, we may be thinking about flavors, texture, nutrition, or price.

Clayton Christensen, author of *The Innovator's Dilemma* and Harvard Business School professor, tells a story about a fast-food chain trying to increase milkshake sales. The company looked at sales data and demographics. They asked target customers to describe their ideal milkshakes and strove to meet those criteria. But sales didn't budge.

Christensen describes what happened when the fast-food chain hired one of his researchers* to take a different approach to figuring out how they could sell more milkshakes.

The researcher discovered that 40% of the milkshakes were purchased first thing in the morning, by commuters who ordered them to go. He interviewed customers who left with milkshake in hand, asking them what job they had hired the milkshake to do.

"Most of them, it turned out, bought [the milkshake] to do a similar job," he writes. *"They faced a long, boring commute and needed something to keep that extra hand busy and to make the commute more interesting. They weren't yet hungry, but knew that they'd be hungry by 10 am; they wanted to consume something now that would stave off hunger until noon. And they faced constraints: They were in a hurry, they were wearing work clothes, and they had (at most) one free hand."*

It might seem odd to ask someone what job she "hired" a milkshake to do, but it successfully shifted the perspective from a focus on the product to the customer's reason for buying the product.

Seeing the problem from the customer's perspective opens up new opportunities. There's a limited number of options when you're trying to make more sellable milkshakes, but many more when you're considering all of the ways in which you could reduce the pain of a hungry, bored, one-handed person.

You could branch into smoothies or coffee shakes, or any food that can be packaged to fit in a cup holder and easily eaten with one hand. You could offer a prepaid commuter card that allowed people to pay in advance (lock-in) and zip through the drive-through line faster. At the same time, it becomes clearer that certain things probably *won't* work: incremental improvements to flavor or texture, reducing the price, or TV advertising.

------

* *http://hbswk.hbs.edu/item/6496.html*. It's worth four minutes to watch Christensen narrate this story himself: *http://www.youtube.com/watch?v= s9nbTB33hbg*.

What You Should Be Listening For

To get the most out of the five basic customer development questions, you'll want to know what to listen for. These are the objective and subjective factors that separate prospective customers from buying customers:

- How your customers are behaving today (which predicts how they'll behave tomorrow)

- The constraints that affect the choices and actions that your customers take

- What frustrates or motivates your customers

- How your customers make decisions, spend money, and determine value

For each of these factors, we'll walk through how they impact decision making and how you can frame your follow-up questions to uncover the most useful details.

Are Interviews Necessary?

For most companies, yes.

Interviews are the fastest, cheapest way to learn more about what your customers are doing and what problems they're facing.

But that may not be the case *if* you already have customers, a product, and the infrastructure to quickly release and evaluate changes.

Dan Levy, Director of Small Business at Facebook, explains, "We can develop a product incredibly quickly, and we have sufficient traffic that we can see if it's working in 15 minutes, including who is using it and how much. Based on that information we can iterate."

Facebook offers a Promoted Posts feature that allows small business advertisers to ensure that a post on their Facebook page is more likely to be seen. The feature drives more than half of new advertiser growth.

Promoted Posts started out as a very powerful tool … with a very high user drop-off. It didn't require talking to customers to form a hypothesis: Small business advertisers are faced with too many choices and fear making a mistake, so they abandon the process.

Levy started by moving the Promoted Posts buying interface from a standalone workflow to a single-button option within the customer's Facebook page. "Everyone already knew how to create a post—now all customers had to do was tell us how much money they wanted to spend. We reduced the complexity from 50 decisions to basically just one."

The result? New advertisers more than doubled in 2013, and 62% of them were acquired through the Promoted Posts channel.

Levy adds that iteration is critical: "A single pivot wasn't enough; the interface still wasn't correct *enough*. It was surprising how much progress we made after the initial solution launched. We continued with a bunch of additional optimizations that continued to increase the effectiveness of the solution. People notice the transformative changes, but don't realize how much the day-to-day optimization compounds and adds up."

You won't get it right on the first try. That's the thing to remember when you find yourself tempted to skip interviews and just build something. For many teams, you may be able to build a quick version in a day or two. But:

- How long will it take you to get that version in front of hundreds (or thousands) of customers?

- How effectively can you measure that customers are using that version?

- If customers are not using it, will you be able to figure out why?

- Then how long will it take to build the next version?

At Facebook's pace, they can test multiple hypotheses within days. That's not realistic for most organizations. Invalidating multiple hypotheses through customer interviews within days *is* feasible for any team, though.

What's the Customer Already Doing?

Discovering what your customer is doing today is the heart of understanding the problem that you're setting out to solve.

What your customers are doing today tells you:

- What they are capable of doing

- What they are comfortable with doing (and why)

- Which decisions they are making

Their current behavior is your competition. It doesn't matter how effective or ineffective their current behavior seems—it's what they are accustomed to and it works (at least to some degree).

You can learn about how customers are behaving today by prompting with, "Tell me about how you do _____" or "Walk me through how you use _____."

Abstract up one level

How you fill in those blanks is important, too. It's critical to define the problem broadly so that you don't prematurely constrain what your potential customers say. If you think you're solving a specific problem, try to move up one level of abstraction and ask the customer about the problem one step up from that.

NOTE

Abstracting up by one level is what allows you to look beyond incremental, easy-to-copy improvements and see opportunities for disruptive change.

For example, don't ask about how someone arranges grocery delivery online; ask about how she feeds her family. Don't ask about how someone uploads and shares files; ask about the last time she worked on a document and needed a coworker's input.

If TiVo had interviewed customers about how they program their VCRs, they might have gotten feedback that drove them to simplify the programming controls and missed the boat on creating the digital video recording industry. In fact, that's exactly what the first attempts at improving the VCR looked like.*

Compare that to asking customers about the time they missed the last 10 minutes of the final episode of *Twin Peaks* or the game-winning play in the Super Bowl—it's easy to imagine how quickly (and emphatically) customers would've told you about the problems that inspired pausing live TV, recording by show name instead of time slot, and fast-forwarding through commercials.

---

* A company called Gemstar created a product called VCR+ that gave each television program a unique 4-digit code. Instead of having to manually input a channel and program a timeslot—which required having your VCR set to the correct time, its own private nightmare—customers could look up the desired program in their TV Guide or local newspaper television listings and key in that code (*http://en.wikipedia.org/wiki/Video_recorder_scheduling_code*). It was an improvement—assuming you hadn't accidentally thrown out your TV listings or misread the 4-digit code or simply forgotten to enter the code before you left for work in the morning.

Focus on procedure, not outcomes

You may be tempted to ask immediately about critical events such as a purchase, a registration, or completion of a key task. Asking an abstract question like "tell me about how..." feels pretty far removed from understanding the critical events that drive success.

But these customer decisions are made in the complex matrix of the environment they're in, the resources they have available, and their capabilities and past experiences. When you understand the factors that go into customers making decisions, it becomes far easier to figure out how to prioritize specifics about making, marketing, and selling a product.

By asking procedural questions, you prompt the customer to tell her story, step by step. This is how you can uncover how she makes sense of her world. She's likely to skip details, or accidentally omit underlying assumptions. When something doesn't make sense, prompt her for an explanation.

For example, your customer may often use "I" and "we" interchangeably. When she's talking about executing on tasks or making decisions, it's important to know exactly who "we" is!

Customer: *"On Sunday night, we look at the calendar and plan the upcoming week..."*

Interviewer: *"Excuse me, when you say 'we', you mean...?"*

Customer: *"Oh, yes. My husband, myself, and my oldest daughter. She's in high school, so she keeps track of many of her activities on her own."*

Interviewer: *"Thanks. So the three of you look at the calendar and..."*

The specific actions that customers take are important, but equally important are the adjacent factors of how, why, when, and with whom. Those are the underlying root causes that make or break products. As your customer talks, be ready to respond with open-ended questions.

Focus on the present, not the future

Ask someone, "In the future, would you do X?" and you'll get an inaccurate answer. Some people will be too polite to say no. Others will give optimistic or socially acceptable answers. (Ask any smoker how often he's told people he plans to quit.)

The choices we make immediately are different from the ones we make in the future; specifically, our future selves are more virtuous. In a study done at the University of Illinois at Urbana-Champaign, people who were asked to choose movies that they'd like to watch in the future chose highbrow or culturally salient films like *Schindler's List* or *The Piano*. But when asked to choose a movie to watch tonight, they opted for more lowbrow choices like *Mrs. Doubtfire* or *Speed.** It's not hard to find echoes of these behaviors in ourselves. We pay for gym memberships but don't go to the gym; we choose a burger tonight and rationalize that we'll eat a salad for lunch tomorrow; we promise that we'll clear up tech debt† in our next software release.

---

* Daniel Read, George Loewenstein, and Shobana Kalyanaraman. "Mixing Virtue and Vice: Combining the Immediacy Effect and the Diversification Heuristic." *Journal of Behavioral Decision Making*. (12) pp. 257–273, 1999.

† Tech debt is a term used in engineering to refer to shortcuts or suboptimal decisions made in coding, often in order to meet a deadline. As with monetary debt, the implication is that there will be consequences if the debt is not paid off in the future.

At Yammer, a small but vocal set of customers have frequently requested that we enhance our topics functionality (which is similar to hashtags on Twitter or Facebook). But when we look at our analytics data, we can confirm that only a tiny percentage of users have ever added a topic or clicked on a topic in another user's post (Figure 4-1).

Figure 4-1. Some customers ask for enhancements to Yammer topic tags, but very few users have ever even attempted to use this feature

We've made multiple attempts to increase topic usage through visual design and functionality changes, but customer behavior remains unchanged. Despite what users promise about their future behavior ("If topics worked better, we'd be able to curate our Yammer network! If we could use topics more, people would use them to build an internal knowledge base!"), the actual usage we see today tells us that most people are not motivated to use this feature.

To get the most accurate answers from your customers, frame your questions to ask about specific events or decisions and focus on the present or recent past. Table 4-1 provides some examples.

Table 4-1. Prompts that yield aspirational responses versus prompts that yield actual responses

Aspirational	Actual
How likely would you be to use _____?	Tell me about the last time you used something like _____.
How often does _____ situation occur?	In the past month, how many times has _____ situation occurred?
How much would it cost your company if _____ happened?	Last time _____ happened, how much did it cost your company?
How would your family react if you decided to _____?	Last time you made a significant decision, how did your family react?

When I was conducting customer development interviews at KISSmetrics, I talked with many startup founders who were highly aspirational about how they'd use data to search for patterns and run split tests to optimize their businesses. But many of them admitted that they were not currently collecting any data beyond a standard Google Analytics installation.

"Tell me about how you measure data for your business *today...*" forced them to describe their current environment and capabilities honestly. That in turn allowed us to focus on the few features that would bring the most value to that set of customers.

What Constraints Are Holding Customers Back?

When we see customers with problems that they haven't been able to solve, we tend to think that the reason is either lack of access ("they just don't have *this* product") or lack of motivation ("they just don't get it"). In other words, if the customer could get his hands on a product that fixed this problem, he'd be all set. Or, if the customer cared enough to challenge the status quo and look for a solution, he'd have figured one out by now.

In reality, customers are influenced by a number of constraints. Not all of them are objective, but that doesn't reduce their impact. You need to understand the type of constraints limiting your customer because they determine which follow-up questions will be valuable, what type of solutions will be attractive, and what type of solutions will ultimately be effective.

Common constraints that I have noticed include:

- Problem is not perceived as a problem
- Lack of awareness of what's possible technologically
- Limited resources (environment, time, budget)
- Cultural or social expectations that limit behaviors

Let's talk through each of these so that you understand why they pose problems and how you can guide users to see past them.

Problem is not perceived as a problem

People naturally focus on the tasks and processes they are most familiar with. When we have a task to complete, our focus is on completing it rather than optimizing *how* we complete it. We don't challenge our assumptions. This is a concept called *functional fixedness*, described by social psychologist

Karl Duncker as "a mental block against using an object in a new way that is required to solve a problem."*

You may be familiar with the classic experiment on functional fixedness. Participants were given a box of tacks, a candle, and a book of matches and challenged to attach the candle to a wall so that no wax dripped to the floor below. The solution requires rethinking the uses for each of those ordinary items. Dump the tacks out of the box and use a tack to attach the box to the wall, forming a "shelf"; then use a bit of candle wax as adhesive to stick the candle to the shelf.

We're not good at this kind of rethinking. In everyday life, the ability to see an object or process as having only one purpose makes our brains more efficient. But that efficiency makes us terrible at coming up with novel solutions to complicated problems.

In the candle and box experiment, the participants knew that they had a specific problem to solve. They were told that a valid solution existed—it was just a matter of figuring out what it was. In real life, we don't always realize that there is a problem. Even when we're experiencing a frustration or lack, we don't realize how bad it is unless we have something to compare it to. In fact, as author Daniel Pink points out, even offering explicit incentives to "think outside the box" doesn't work.[†]

Take online shoe shopping. Many people won't buy shoes without trying them on because it's hard to get the right fit—even if you're buying the same brand and size that you've worn for years. Shoefitr is a Pittsburgh-based company that uses 3D imaging to measure the internal dimensions of shoes.[‡] The customer can look at the measurements of a shoe he's browsing and compare them to the shoes that are already on his feet.

When user researcher Grace O'Malley talked to customers, they described different strategies for getting the right shoe size. O'Malley explains, "Some people would buy multiple pairs in different sizes and return the ones that didn't fit. A lot of people would just make a shoe work, by putting insoles in or in other scrappy ways. They just dealt with it. Some refused to buy shoes online. But no one asked for a solution that would help you find the shoes that would fit your feet in advance of buying them."

---

* *http://en.wikipedia.org/wiki/Functional_fixedness*

† *http://www.ted.com/talks/dan_pink_on_motivation.html*

‡ According to online running shoe retailer Running Warehouse, 65% of all returned shoes were due to improper fit. In the first two years of using Shoefitr, fit-related returns fell by 23%, which resulted in a 2.5% increase in profit margins (*http://www.runblogrun.com/2012/05/shoefitr-use-of-online-fitting-application-increases-rate-of-returns-decreases-release-from-shoe-fit.html*).

You need customers to realize that they have a problem so that they can critique possible solutions. One way to do this is to make them think more deeply about behaviors that have become routine.

For example, when I worked at Yodlee, an online banking solution provider, I spent a lot of time thinking about the problems around online bill payment. One thing I noticed was that people use a lot of mental shorthand: we say "paying bills online" to refer to a collection of activities that may include circling due dates on a physical calendar, calculating balances, confirming which checks have cleared, and resetting a forgotten password as well as the quick step of confirming payment accounts and clicking Submit on the banking website.

Tony McCaffrey, CTO at Innovation Accelerator, uses what he calls the "generic parts technique."* "Break each object into its parts and ask two questions," says McCaffrey. "Can it be broken down further? Does your description imply a use? If so, describe it more generically."

In my experience, when customers talked about paying bills online, they were satisfied with how long they spent on the activity. When they broke that familiar activity into its component generic parts, it made them stop and question the amount of time and effort they expended on the task.

When your customers describe their behaviors, you want them to realize that every action and assumption that is second nature is actually a decision that they are making—and that better options may exist.

Another way is to challenge the unrealized problem is to create some implied comparisons between what the customer's life is like now and what it would be like in a future where his problem is solved. This doesn't mean that you should talk about the specifics of your product! Instead, you'll want to dig into how the problem is causing pain to the customer. Is it wasting an hour of his time that he'd rather spend with his family? Is it costing an amount of money equivalent to what he spends on gas each week? Is it creating social friction that's hurting a relationship?

Lack of awareness of what's technologically possible

Problems without conceivable solutions feel more like facts than problems. It may not occur to people to complain about something if they believe that there is no way it can be remedied. The solutions we suggest are rooted in

---

* *http://blogs.hbr.org/cs/2012/05/overcoming_functional_fixednes.html*

what we perceive as possible. This is why customers tend to suggest incremental improvements rather than fundamental changes.

As the people who build products, we're immersed in our worlds. We're familiar with what technology and process and automation can do. Our customers are not.

Think about a solution like Siri. Just a couple of years ago, most people's experience with voice recognition was limited to those nightmarish automated interactive voice response systems where you find yourself yelling *"1, ENGLISH, NO, 3, TALK TO OPERATOR, OPERATOR, OPERATOR!"* at your phone and then hanging up in disgust. How could a customer ask for anything resembling Siri if that was her only experience with natural-language processing and voice recognition?

Even when a customer can conceive of a solution that doesn't exist today, she's unlikely to share it for fear of sounding foolish. We don't want to admit that we can't tell the difference between something difficult and something impossible. Who wants the embarrassment of inadvertently asking for something ridiculous?*

It's not easy to get customers to think outside the realm of what they know is possible, but it can be done.

There's a question that I'll reference throughout this book, and it's this: *"Forget about what's possible. If you could wave a magic wand and solve anything, what would you do?"*

The magic wand question takes a huge burden off your customer's shoulders. It tells him that he doesn't have to worry about what is possible. There are no wrong answers. When you frame the interview in this way, you tend to hear, "Well, this is ridiculous but…" followed by legitimate problems and creative ideas. The ideas that customers propose are usually not possible or practical, but they can lead you to ones that are.

"I wish I could just sit on people's shoulders—like the devil on their shoulder—and ask 'Why?' right at the moment when they abandon my website." That response to the magic wand question helped KISSmetrics

---

* This fear is wonderfully captured in the goofy movie *Austin Powers: The Spy Who Shagged Me*, when Dr. Evil has traveled back in time to 1969 and is threatening the President:

Dr. Evil: "Mr. President, after I destroy Washington, D.C…I will destroy another major city every hour on the hour. That is, unless of course you pay me… [dramatic pause] one hundred billion dollars."

His request is so ridiculous that his audience, instead of cowering in fear, bursts out laughing at him: "Dr. Evil, this is 1969! That amount of money doesn't even exist! That's like saying, I want a kajillion bajillion dollars!"

design KISSinsights, an on-site survey tool. It perfectly captured the frustration that our customers were feeling.

Limited resources

Sometimes customers are constrained by the environment they are working or living in. People living in dorms or apartments or working in cubicles may not be able to take advantage of a solution that requires them to make changes to their physical space. Parents of young children may not be able to benefit from a solution that requires two hands or rapt concentration. (Product designer Anne Halsall writes, "For the first three weeks of our son's life, I didn't touch a computer I couldn't use with one hand…an iPad mini immediately became my primary computer.")*

Many environmental limitations are not permanent. Consider noise, poor weather, crowded physical space, unreliable Internet access, or the distance between points A and B. They simply add a small amount of additional friction, which is often enough to inhibit customer behaviors.

Of course, most customers face some sort of resource constraints. It's critical to understand *which* resources are scarce. A busy working parent is less likely to spend time in order to save money; a college student often has the opposite inclination. At KISSmetrics, many of our early customers had limited engineering resources. This meant that they were willing to trade a shorter installation and setup process for a longer one that could be accomplished mostly by nonengineers.

Cultural or social expectations that limit behaviors

At Yammer, we often encounter users with a set of internal rules for how they use our product: "I read all the time, but I only respond to a question if it's asked by one of my peers. I'm not comfortable responding to managers."

There are no limitations in the software. It's even unlikely that their particular company has articulated guidelines on who talks with whom. That doesn't matter. A hierarchical work culture can influence behavior even if the rules are entirely unspoken.

---

* This story is so good that I have to quote some more from it: "What I realized was that before I became a parent, I never really thought about the one-armed people of the world. And by that I simply mean the people who, because of their work or the circumstances of their lives, don't have much of an opportunity to use any device that requires two hands. Once you start looking for these people you see them everywhere… They don't use devices unless they are small and light enough to be operated one-handed. Parents of small children certainly fall into this category. So do people with active jobs who are often standing or traveling" (*http://contextsensitive.quora.com/Seeking-the-one-armed-man*).

Does your customer feel that she will be judged negatively if she tries your solution and it is not successful? If so, how can you reduce her sense of risk in decision making? Does your customer feel that she needs permission before changing behaviors? If so, you'll want to focus heavily on the other stakeholders who she perceives as granting that permission. (See "How Your Customers Make Decisions, Spend Money, and Determine Value" later in this chapter.)

Another cultural obstacle is that a product may conflict with how the customer wishes to view herself.

A couple years ago, I was working with a startup team that wanted to solve the problem of people losing expensive items. They asked people in their personal networks if they knew anyone who was always losing things and quickly found dozens of professionals who routinely lost iPhones, laptops, ski equipment, and other expensive items. The interviewees admitted that they wasted hours each week and spent hundreds or even thousands of dollars replacing lost items.

But when the team started investigating how much these prospective customers were willing to spend on a solution, they ran into resistance. One customer finally admitted, "I've just gotten used to budgeting extra money to replace the stuff I'll inevitably lose. I'm OK with that."

Even if you objectively know that you lost your laptop last month and your keys twice this week, you may not think of yourself as a careless person. Buying a product to keep you from losing things is akin to admitting that you are.

This is a great example of where Steve Blank's earlyvangelist diagram in Chapter 3 should be keeping you honest. These customers may have seemed ideal, but they were not actively seeking a solution. Time to pivot and seek out a different target audience.

Social and cultural limitations aren't always obvious to your customer, either. Sometimes customers are fully aware that they don't want to, or would be uncomfortable, using your product. Often they are not. Try asking the customer to envision herself fixing the problem, and watch for body language or changes in her tone of voice. Does she seem relieved or excited at the prospect of fixing the problem? Or does she seem hesitant or conflicted?

What Frustrates (or Motivates) Your Customer?

People are not strictly rational. Our decisions are not based solely on logical, economic criteria. We choose more expensive options because they look cooler; we reject potential solutions because something about them makes us feel uncomfortable.

As your potential customers describe what they're doing today, listen carefully for hints of what frustrates them and what motivates them.

Why?

No matter how effective your product or service is, it still requires effort and investment from the customer. To maintain that effort and investment, your customer needs positive feedback. What motivates one customer may turn off another. You'll need to uncover what incentivizes your customer as well as what types of frustration he considers a deal-breaker.

One of the biggest demotivators that I've run across, in multiple contexts, is uncertainty. Being unsure of how a service will work, or how to best interact with a product, creates such a high level of discomfort that customers may choose to disengage. This specific issue is worth exploring because it creates a big disconnect for us.

As people who envision and build new products, we tend to be unusually comfortable with uncertainty. Our customers are not.

"How does it work? How should I use it? What will happen if I...?" are the first questions that people ask every time I introduce them to a new feature.

You'll also want to figure out what makes your customer feel successful. Is he motivated by mastering a task, by seeing visible progress, or by performing a task better than his peers?

The incentives you provide should align with what your customer values. For customers who are competitive, earning a spot atop a leaderboard is motivating. It does little to nothing for customers who value hearing "thank you" from someone they've helped.

How Your Customers Make Decisions, Spend Money, and Determine Value

The person who uses the product isn't always the one who buys it. Toys and clothing are used by kids and purchased by parents. Medicines and medical devices are used by patients, prescribed by doctors, and (typically) paid for by medical insurance. But the relationship between the primary user and the other invisible stakeholders—people or organizations that make decisions or have influence—is not always that clear.

You'll want to ask which people or groups have this problem directly and which experience it secondhand. If the customer doesn't mention anyone else, you can try asking about which other people are present when the problem occurs, or which other people they discuss the problem with.

Common invisible stakeholders include:

- Kids and spouse (desire to minimize conflict)
- Social circle (desire to avoid judgment)
- Whoever holds the checkbook/credit card/purchase requisition forms
- People who provide scarce and needed skills, such as an engineering team or legal counsel
- People who ensure compliance, such as IT security, finance, or legal counsel
- People who use the product with the customer (for products that require collaboration or a network effect)

Looking Objectively at Subjective Qualities

I mentioned an apparent contradiction earlier in this chapter: you need to ask objective questions, but you need to elicit subjective and personal answers.

Don't interpret that as meaning that you need to ask about personal characteristics directly. You're likely to insult someone if you ask about her level of tech savvy or how price-sensitive she is. Even if the interviewee didn't find your question rude, she's going to give you an answer based on what she knows of herself and her immediate social circle. In other words, if she's the only one of her friends who goes to the gym, she's going to rate herself as athletic even if she couldn't finish a 5K to save her life.

Instead, extrapolate the details of what your customers are like from the hints that they drop in their responses. For example, what can you deduce from someone who mentions, "Oh yeah, I tried an app to help me do that"? That sentence reveals that she:

- Has a smartphone
- Has demonstrated the initiative to look for apps to solve her problems
- Is capable of finding and downloading the app

This may feel like pretty advanced deduction, but as you talk with more customers, it will become second nature. You'll begin to notice subtle differences ("I tried an app to help me" versus "My kids put this app on my phone to help me") that tell you a lot about your customers.

In Chapter 2, we talked about creating a traits continuum to flesh out the details of what you believe your target customer looks and acts like. Now let's think about a blank version of that canvas. For the traits at each end, what types of behaviors or word choices help us figure out more about this customer (Figure 4-3)?

A customer who mentions being late or trying to fit in workouts might belong closer to the "values time" end of the spectrum. Saying "I hate it when my coworkers do things out of order" hints at a person who is willing to sacrifice some efficiency or ease of use in exchange for predictability. I don't use traits continuums in every interview anymore, but looking at one is helpful when you're just getting started. What may seem like throwaway comments are actually valuable clues to what motivates this person to try and buy.

Figure 4-3. A traits continuum

Next Step: Get Ready to Do Your Customer Development Interviews

This chapter may have felt a bit dense and theoretical, but we're about to head back into tactical territory. In the next chapter, we'll walk through the interview to give you a sense of how it flows and what to be prepared for. After you read Chapter 5, you'll be ready to get out of the building.

Key Takeaways

- Use the five basic customer development questions to get customers talking—then ask them for more details about their answers.

- Ask open-ended questions so that customers go beyond the surface.

- Find out what they're doing today. Their current behavior is your competition.

- Abstract up a level to get perspective.

- Focus on actual versus aspirational behavior. Instead of asking, "How likely would you be to *X*?", ground your prompts in the recent past ("Tell me about the last time you..." or "In the past month, how many times ...").

- Be aware of mental blocks customers may have (not perceiving the problem as a problem, thinking it can't be fixed, having limited resources, having expectations that limit their behaviors) and ask questions to help move beyond those blocks.

- Find out if there are other stakeholders involved in making decisions (family, managers, friends, etc.).

CHAPTER 5

Get Out of the Building

After a short intro, I was able to transition [the interview] to just two people talking on the phone. People were staying far longer than the requested 10 minutes, and I was learning far more than I could have in any other format.

—Nick Soman, CEO of LikeBright

Great products require deep human empathy: you can't solve for that without talking to the customer early and often. Sitting behind a glass wall and having people do things on a computer—how realistic is that? We should be having conversations with people.

—Kara DeFrias, Innovation Catalyst at Intuit

You've written down your hypotheses, found people to talk to, figured out what you need to learn, devised questions to get you there, and scheduled a time.

Now comes the hard part: actually doing your first interview.

I'm going to be honest: I dreaded the first few customer interviews I did.

What if I don't learn anything useful? What if this feels like a bad first date with long, awkward silences? What if my interviewee feels like I'm wasting her time?

Thousands of interviews later, I've learned that you control the tone of the conversation. When you speak confidently, set expectations appropriately, and express genuine curiosity, people talk. When you close with heartfelt appreciation, you build a relationship and people are happy to talk with you again in the future. I still keep in touch with a couple dozen people I met through customer development interviews.

This chapter gives you the tools to create comfortable and constructive interviews. As we walk through the interview process play-by-play, we'll cover effective tactics and explain why they work. You'll learn:

- How to prepare before the interview
- The surprising trick that gets people to open up and talk freely
- How to give people permission to be experts
- Why you should embrace tangents
- The value of thanking people using the foot-in-the-door method

At the end of this chapter, you'll have all the tools you need to get out of the building and learn some surprising, insightful, and unexpected things from your interviews.

The Practice Interview

Every interview after the first is easier. For that reason, I recommend doing a practice interview with someone you know who is not one of your target customers.

A practice interview won't validate your hypotheses, but it will give you the opportunity to test the process and improve your interview techniques before moving on to real subjects.

The practice interview can also be helpful if you already have a product and customers. Sometimes you'll need greater sensitivity when talking about hypothetical ideas with people who've already written you a check, and it helps to walk through that in advance with someone who understands (i.e., a colleague, not the customer).*

---

* A lot of things about customer development may change if you're working with existing customers, but not the fundamental psychology of how to get people to talk. We'll talk about those changes and risks in Chapter 8. I recommend reading this chapter first and then thinking about how to adapt what you learn to your situation.

Who should you interview for this dry run? While your practice interviewee doesn't need to meet any particular criteria, it's a good idea to choose someone who isn't too closely related to your idea. It can be challenging to keep a straight face if you interview your partner or best friend. A more distant coworker, or a nonstale LinkedIn connection, may be a better choice.

At Yammer, my team often tests interviews on new hires who aren't yet familiar with the interviewer or the product. No special instructions are needed; we just tell them to answer the questions based on their own experiences or opinions. After the interview, we ask them for feedback on the interview itself. That's a good idea, no matter who you choose for your practice interview.

To Record or Not to Record?

You might wonder, "What about making an audio recording of my interviews?" If you're thinking of recording, you may be worried that you can't write or type quickly enough to capture verbatim comments, or that the conversation will feel awkward because you are writing instead of making eye contact with your interviewee.

Here are some pros and cons of recording the audio of your interviews:

Pros:

- You'll capture everything your interviewee says.

- You won't inadvertently bias your notes (writing down a milder or summarized version of what the interviewee said).

- You can focus on body language and facial expressions.

- Playing back audio from a real person speaking, with pauses and intonation, is more powerful than sharing a verbatim quote.

Cons:

- Asking if you may record the conversation is an awkward beginning to the interview.

- Recording interviews effectively doubles the amount of time per interview since you need to go back and listen to the interview a second time to capture notes or excerpts.

- Interviewees may be more cautious when they know they are being recorded. (And no, recording without their permission is not an acceptable workaround.)

- Employees may be subject to their employer's legal restrictions, even if they're not talking about their own products or processes.

- Taking notes manually (by hand or typing) is a valuable hack to keep you from talking, encouraging interviewees to talk more.

The right approach is the one that helps you run effective interviews. You'll probably want to try both ways to figure out which you prefer.

The format of your interviews may influence how you decide to capture notes. I conduct most of my customer development interviews over the phone, where no one can see that my eyes keep flicking back to my laptop screen. However, I don't feel comfortable typing into a laptop during a face-to-face interview. While working on this book, I've discovered that I can no longer write by hand fast enough to capture verbatim quotes. I just don't write by hand often enough to maintain that speed!

Whether you record your conversations or take manual notes, though, you'll need to spend a few minutes after each interview synthesizing the highlights. If you leave your notes untouched and come back several days later, it won't matter whether they're three pages of handwriting or 30 minutes of voice recording—either will be unapproachable!

No Video Please

I don't recommend video recording, even though it is common practice in usability testing. Although a video clip is highly effective in convincing even the most skeptical coworker, it's also incredibly constraining. It requires a camera-friendly location, which is usually not a human-friendly location. For remote interviews, it requires your interviewee to have a webcam and know how to set it up—hardly something most of us can count on. It's also just plain awkward: who can loosen up and feel like an expert when they're worried about how their hair looks on camera?

Taking Great Notes

Taking notes during customer development interviews requires something that might at first seem strange. I want you to forget everything you know about note-taking from school or from meetings.

If you take notes in that style, you're wasting your time. When you take notes in a lecture or during a meeting, you summarize. You make deliberate choices to omit some points, condense others, and translate some of what you hear into what you *think* the speaker was actually trying to say. If you're taking notes in a work meeting, you may have to share them with a wider audience and sanitize or contextualize what you write accordingly.

When you're doing customer development, *you don't know what's important yet.* You won't know what's important until after you've completed a number of interviews.

It's critical to capture as much information as possible—in high-fidelity, with details, emotion, and exclamation points. If your interviewee says, "Using product X is literally the worst part of my entire week," that is *not* the same as "Customer doesn't like product X."

Obviously you can't write down every word. (You probably don't want to, either; at some point you have to go back and read all these notes.) As a guide, remember that you're using what you learn to validate hypotheses and find out more about your target customers' pains. You need the most detail when the interviewee says:

- Something that validates your hypothesis

- Something that invalidates your hypothesis

- Anything that takes you by surprise

- Anything full of emotion

When you hear any of these things, mark them emphatically in your notes. Circle them, bold them, or highlight them to ensure they stand out later. If you're recording the audio of the interview, write down timestamps when any of these interest points occur so that you can easily reference that portion of the conversation later.

People often ask, "Why is emotion so important? What if the person is just complaining about something unrelated to my product idea?" *Emotion—* and by that, I mean complaining, anger, enthusiasm, disgust, skepticism, embarrassment, frustration—*is prioritization.* If you want to know what's important to someone, don't ask them for a list: you'll hear what they intellectually think *ought* to be important to them. Instead, listen for emotion when they talk. Those are the areas of opportunity. Even if what they are saying seems unrelated to your product idea, it will help you flesh out a greater understanding of your target customer.

Another note-taking challenge is that every conversation flows differently. (If your interviews don't, you aren't letting customers drive the conversation enough.) But you'll eventually need to be able to compare across dozens of conversations. You can make this easier by using a template for taking notes for each interview.

Your template should be flexible enough to work for a variety of conversations, but structured enough to ensure you cover the most critical three or four questions with each interviewee. I've also found it useful to include some reminders to myself about what to do and what not to do on my template (see Figure 5-1).

Name: _____   Smile
Date: _____
                                        STOP TALKING,
                                        you're just the notetaker

Tell me about how you do _____ today...   No yes/no questions

                                        Restate anything
Do you use any other tools or have any specific tips or tricks   interesting back to
you use to help?   the person

                                        Other people...

Is there anything specific that you always do before or after
you do _____?

If you could wave a magic wand and be able to do anything else
that you can't do today, what would it be? (Forget about whether
or not it's possible, just anything.)

Also interesting:

Figure 5-1. My interview template, which has a few of my most commonly asked questions, with reminders to myself on the right (because I typically do phone interviews, I can type directly into the template)

Invite a Note-taker

At Yammer, when we do customer development interviews, we improve the interviewer's ability to focus on the interview itself by inviting a second person to take notes (see "Pair Interviewing" on the next page).

Inviting someone to take notes is a great way to get people from other cross-functional teams in front of customers! We have coworkers who would never agree to conduct an interview but who are willing to help us out by taking notes. (This is not to say there wasn't initial resistance to taking notes for us. We needed home-baked cookies to entice our initial volunteers. But after about six months, we are now able to require at least one hour of note-taking participation from everyone on our product teams.)

We use an online note-taking template with the sections already described: validates, invalidates, surprising, and emotions. The note-taker brings his laptop into the room and types directly into the template. This way, notes are in a consistent format, searchable, and no one needs to transcribe.

Pair Interviewing

One of the most effective practices that I've used at Yammer and KISSmetrics is to conduct interviews in pairs. One person conducts the interview, asking the questions and maintaining eye contact while the other focuses on taking notes.

In addition to yielding more comprehensive and useful notes, this method has three other key benefits:

Your interviews improve

When you are talking, it is extremely difficult to recognize when you've spoken too much, asked a leading question, or ended a line of conversation prematurely. It's much more obvious to your colleague taking notes. She can give you feedback immediately after the interview is over, which allows you to keep improving your interview technique.

Helps convince others to interview

In many cases, you're likely to have team members who are either skeptical of customer development or think it's beneficial but don't want to do it themselves. It's easier to get them to commit to a half-hour of note-taking than asking them to build a new skill. After a couple note-taking sessions, I will typically ask a colleague, "So, do you want to run the interview yourself next time?"

Helps you include everyone on your team

In many companies, there are people who are always too busy, too far away, or too uncomfortable to effectively talk to customers. Unfortunately, these are often the people who most need to hear an outside perspective. If I can only get an hour of a colleague's time, the most effective way I can use that is to schedule her for two half-hour note-taking sessions. It's a low-energy commitment that doesn't require advance preparation, but gives colleagues the benefit of hearing firsthand from two different people outside our office.

Immediately Before the Interview

Familiarize yourself with the person you're about to talk to. If you're targeting someone in the workplace, look at her job title, the type of company she works for, and the industry she's in. If you're targeting a consumer, look at whether she's single or married with kids, suburban or urban, tech-savvy or not. Take a minute to put yourself in her shoes and think about the types of things she's likely to think and worry about.

During your conversation, you're likely to make ad hoc references or give examples. Your interviewee will feel more comfortable, and be more willing to talk freely, if he can relate to those references.* (For example, a single guy who lives in the city is less likely to relate to a reference about shuttling kids around in an SUV.)

Don't forget the *really* mundane. Use the restroom. Get a drink of water. Have extra pens and paper on hand. Your phone should be charged and silenced. If you're typing, remove all distractions. Close your IM client, your browsers, your email, and get rid of any other potential distractions. (I usually disable my WiFi.) Get your note-taking template in front of you and get ready to start writing or typing!

The First Minute

As you dial your interviewee's number or wait for her to arrive, you probably feel a bit nervous and unsure about what to expect. So does the person you're about to interview.

Most people have never done anything like a customer development interview before. Even if they've participated in usability testing or traditional marketing focus groups, those follow quite a different format. Usability testing and focus groups have more structure and moderation. Both are typically oriented around an existing product, service, or prototype. Because you kept your initial interview request brief, your interviewee isn't entirely sure what to expect.

It's your job, in the first minute of your conversation, to do three things:

- Make the interviewee feel confident that she will be helpful

- Explicitly say that you want her to do the talking

- Get the interviewee talking (I'll explain how)

The beginning and the end of the interview are the only times where I recommend that you rehearse what you're going to say in advance. Having a

---

* Zappos's customer support attempts to create a personal emotional connection on every support call. Geographical call routing attempts to connect you to a support professional in the same location to increase the odds that you'll have something in common. This emotional connection is one of the reasons why 75% of Zappos's business is repeat business from existing customers. For you, fostering this connection will help some interviewees become your cheerleaders and advisors.

script for the beginning of your interviews helps you to sound confident and set expectations appropriately. A good opening script for a phone interview might look like this:

Hello, this is [Name] from [Company]. Is this still a good time to talk?

Great! First of all, I'd like to thank you for talking with me today. It's incredibly valuable for me to get to listen to you talk me through your personal experience and how things work (and don't work) in your world, so I'll mostly be listening.

Could you start by telling me a bit about how you [perform general task] currently?

Sounds pretty basic, but there are some very specific elements that make this an effective opening. Every time I've deviated from these, or worked with a company that has, the quality of responses goes down. Those elements include:

Keeping the tone conversational

If you're from a conservative industry, like finance or healthcare, you may think that this introduction is too casual and that you'll need to adopt a more formal tone. What I've found is that using more formal terms correlates with shorter, more sanitized answers. If you're talking to an employee, you don't want to hear the official process; you need to know all the secret grumblings and workarounds that people have patched together to get their jobs done. Those are the insights you need to build an incredible product. Talk the way you'd talk in the break room, not the way you'd speak in an executive presentation.

Being human

When you're talking, use "I" and "me," not "we" or "company." People are more likely to help someone they have a connection with than a faceless "we" or company. Social psychology research bears this out.*

Emphasizing the personal

Using phrases like "your personal experiences," "for you, specifically," or "in your world" may feel awkward at first. However, it helps emphasize that the interviewee is the expert and that his specific opinions and

---

* This is probably due to the relationship between self-disclosure and likeability: people who reveal personal information about themselves are more often liked by others (*http://www. ncbi.nlm.nih.gov/pubmed/7809308*). Even if all you reveal is your name and enough personality to demonstrate that you're not reading a script, that's probably sufficient.

behaviors are valuable. It's very common to hear people demur, "Oh, I'm just an ordinary [fill-in-the-blank]; you can't be interested in what I have to say." You need to help the interviewee overcome that hesitancy in order to draw out detailed answers.

As long as you preserve those elements, you can (and should!) adapt your opening to fit your personal speaking style and your company.

The Next Minute

You've just finished your opening script and explained how vital it is that your interviewee—the expert—share everything he knows. Here's what will naturally happen: your interviewee doesn't want to dominate the conversation (even though you just encouraged him to do so!). He'll say one or two sentences and stop.

How do you convince someone to violate our ingrained social norms and keep talking?

You shut up and listen. You say your opening bit, you ask the first "Tell me about how you…" question, and you wait. Look at the clock and don't say another word for a full *60 seconds* (Figure 5-2).

Figure 5-2. Wait a full 60 seconds after you ask the first question

Sixty seconds is a long time. You will want to say something to break the silence or move to the next question. Don't. By jumping in too quickly, you signal that the interviewee has said enough and that you're not interested in hearing more. He will take your attempt to break the silence as an indicator that one or two sentences is the right level of detail and will start giving you short, shallow answers. That's not what you want at all!

Instead of talking, let the silence happen.

I recently saw a tweet that suggested literally hitting the mute button on the phone to prevent yourself from talking. I actually don't recommend this: it's noticeable when the other end of the line goes completely silent, and it sounds like a dropped call. You don't want your interviewee to interrupt themselves to ask, "Hello? Are you still there? Did I lose you?" Keep the subtle sounds of you breathing and listening audible.

If you remain quiet, most people will then continue to talk,* and it's usually those details—not the summary—that contain the useful insights. (If your interviewee doesn't start talking again, or seems genuinely uncomfortable, you may need to provide a verbal nudge. Typically you won't need to.)

Forcing him to keep the conversation going in the first exchange sets the tone. You really meant what you said; you are mostly going to listen. Now your interviewee knows that it's OK to give long, detailed descriptions.

Keeping the Conversation Flowing

After the initial "tell me about how" question, your interview can be as freeform as needed.

You may find yourself asking each question on your list in turn or spending 10 minutes on a single question because your interviewee can't stop talking about it.

The most important thing is to keep your interviewee talking and subtly encourage her to go into more detail about the things that she gets most excited about.

WARNING

Don't keep doing the "stay quiet for 60 seconds" trick. It works incredibly well to kick off your interview the right way, but it can feel cold or manipulative if you overuse it. Pausing to ensure that you don't interrupt or cut off your interviewee is good, but you can keep the pauses to two or three seconds. Once you've got a person talking, you want to make him feel like the expert. That requires you to be an active listener—acknowledging what the person is saying and asking questions.

---

* I'm sure there's a legitimate social psychology reason for this, but I'll cite *Pulp Fiction* instead:
  Mia: *Don't you hate that?*
  Vincent: *Hate what?*
  Mia: *Uncomfortable silences. Why do we feel it's necessary to yak about bullshit? In order to be comfortable?*
  Vincent: *That's a good question.*

Keep asking questions to draw out as much detail as possible. You want to encourage longer answers. The best prompts are open-ended and don't lend themselves to a yes-or-no response:

- How long does that process take?

- Why do you think that happens?

- What's the consequence of that happening?

- Who else is involved with decisions like this?

- Where else do you see this kind of mistake?

- When was the last time you did that task?

Asking this type of follow-up question doesn't just keep the person talking; it can entirely change the tone of his response. Read this exchange from an early interviewee with KISSmetrics, a web analytics company:

> **Customer:** *We're already using some analytics tools that our engineers built custom, and that seems to work fine. We can see conversions and traffic and get reports when we need them.*

This seems like an uninterested customer. He's telling me he already has a solution to his pain point. He isn't expressing frustration. He isn't complaining about things he can't do.

Time to move on to the next question? Not so fast. You'll want to ask at least one follow-up question to make sure that there's nothing interesting here:

> **Interviewer:** *You said you can get reports when you need them. When's the last time you needed a report?*
>
> **Customer:** *Last week. Well... we could've used some data last week, but actually the engineer who runs the reports was in the middle of fixing some big bug, so I had to wait a couple days to get it.*
>
> **Interviewer:** *How often does that happen, that you need some data but have to wait to get it?*
>
> **Customer:** *Well, it happened last week. And probably a couple times this month. But it's more important for engineers to be working on bug fixes or features than to run reports. [long pause] Yeah... I guess I end up making decisions based on my best guess instead of having numbers.*
>
> **Interviewer:** *How important do you think those decisions are? What is the consequence of not having those numbers?*

Customer: *Honestly, it hasn't been that important with what we've done so far. But we're about to make some changes that directly affect monetization. If we make wrong guesses there, we lose money. Pretty direct connection. Ugh! I've been so busy I hadn't thought about this yet, but this is really urgent....*

Avoiding Leading Questions

Be careful with your follow-up questions. It is very easy to accidentally ask leading questions. Once you've asked a leading question, you have biased your interviewee's response. Leading questions are often constructed like:

- Don't you think _____?
- Would it cause a problem if _____?
- Would you agree that _____?
- Would you like it if _____?

This structure often leads to the interviewee starting his answer with "yes" or "no." You may not realize that you just asked a leading question, but if your interviewee starts an answer with "yes" or "no," you probably did. Mark it down in your notes so you know to treat that answer with skepticism.

Of course, there will be plenty of occasions where the interviewee isn't saying anything interesting even after you've nudged him some more with follow-up questions. Don't force it. Not every question is productive for every person. Move on to your next question or topic.

Digging a Little Deeper

At the end of a long series of questions, you may think you understand a specific situation or problem. Your instinct will be to simply agree, saying "yes" or "I get it." Don't do that just yet. There will often be some detail you misunderstood or that the interviewee omitted. Instead, ask for clarity. A good format is to state what you're doing, summarize what the person said in your own words, and explicitly ask her to correct you. I recommend restating the interviewee's words any time she says something particularly interesting (or surprising), as well as at the end of a series of questions before you move on to another topic.

Summarizing what the person said back to her can feel awkward, even condescending. (Just the phrase "active listening" conjures up memories of well-meaning kindergarten teachers or old Stuart Smalley sketches on *Saturday Night Live*.) You may be tempted to skip this step because it feels unnatural. Summarizing what the interviewee says gets easier, and you'll save yourself a lot of misunderstandings.

Here's an example from a recent interview with a Yammer user:

> **Me:** *I want to make sure I'm clear on this: you're saying that you send files over email because it's hard to log in to the secure intranet file-sharing site, because it's easier to send them via email. And you share files over email about twice a week? Did I get any of that wrong?*

> **Interviewee:** *No—I mean, I do have problems with the login thing, but the main reason we use email is that our sales guys are always on the road and they can't get to the intranet; they can only get to their email.*

> *So we have to use email. That happens maybe twice a week, except for the end of the quarter, when all of sales is racing to get deals done and then we're sending, like, 20 files over email every day.*

In her response, the interviewee actually identified a different and more important problem! She also realized that this isn't just an everyday pain point; it gets worse at specific high-priority intervals.

These are exactly the type of details that a person wouldn't usually reveal in her initial answers. Interviewees aren't trying to hold back information; they just haven't thought about it from an outsider's perspective before.*

Be Diplomatic with "Why?"

Developed at Toyota, the "5 Whys" is a technique for drilling past surface answers to the root cause of a problem. Most people, when asked a question, gravitate to the most immediately apparent response. That response is usually a symptom, and if we solve for that symptom, we're ignoring the greater opportunity of fixing the root cause.

---

* Or they're suffering, as we all do, from the "curse of knowledge." People who build products become so familiar with those products that they assume that everyone knows how to perform a task or find a feature. People who use products assume that everyone understands how those products are flawed and how they fail to align with how people really work. As author Cynthia Barton Rabe says, "When experts have to slow down and go back to basics to bring an outsider up to speed, it forces them to look at their world differently and, as a result, they come up with new solutions to old problems" (quoted in "Innovative Minds Don't Think Alike" by Janet Rae Dupree, *http://www.nytimes.com/2007/12/30/business/30know.html*).

Here's an example from Eric Ries's blog:

> Let's say you notice that your website is down. Obviously, your first priority is to get it back up. But as soon as the crisis is past, you have the discipline to have a postmortem in which you start asking why:
>
> - Why was the website down? The CPU utilization on all our front-end servers went to 100%.
> - Why did the CPU usage spike? A new bit of code contained an infinite loop!
> - Why did that code get written? So-and-so made a mistake.
> - Why did his mistake get checked in? He didn't write a unit test for the feature.
> - Why didn't he write a unit test? He's a new employee, and he was not properly trained in test-driven development.*

After the first why, it sounds like a hardware issue. After the third why, it'd be tempting to blame the engineer. After the fifth why, it becomes clear that the way to prevent this from happening again is to plug the leaks in the employee onboarding process.

---

* http://www.startuplessonslearned.com/2008/11/five-whys.html

Tangents Happen

The open-ended nature of these interviews means that your interviewee will spend some time talking about seemingly unrelated problems or situations. "Why is he talking about *this* instead of what I want him to be talking about?" you'll wonder.

That's a question worth exploring. Why is this person talking about a seemingly unrelated topic? If a person brings up a topic, it's probably because it's important to him. Maybe it represents a more pressing problem that you should be solving instead. It could be a necessary precondition, something he needs to worry about before he can think about your idea. It might reveal that this person is not the person you should be talking to.

Instead of redirecting the interviewee back to your question, I recommend taking at least a minute or two to explore the tangent. Some questions that may be useful are:

- Do you spend more time on [tangent] or on [original idea]?

- How many people are involved in doing/thinking about/approving/fixing [tangent]?

- How high a priority is [tangent] in your home/workplace?

If it's clear that the interviewee devotes more time and priority to the tangent, you may ask him to refer another interviewee. (Please don't insult the interviewee by asking if there is someone better to talk with—you never know when you may want to revisit a past interviewee.) Here's one way to make that request:

> *Right now, my plan is to focus on [original idea] more than [tangent], so I don't want to take up too much of your time. If I do end up thinking more about [tangent] in the future, can I get back in touch with you?*

> *One last question: if I wanted to learn more about [original idea], do you know someone I should talk to?*

Even if you initially think that a tangent is unimportant, you won't really know for sure until you've talked to enough people to start seeing patterns. When I did customer interviews for KISSmetrics, many people veered away from talking about analytics to complain about how difficult it was for them to do qualitative user research and surveys. When the first person said this, it seemed like an outlier. Once five more people talked about the same problem, and then more, it was clearly an opportunity. (One of my more popular lines in conference talks is "One person might just be a nutcase. Ten people are not all nutcases.") That tangent was the inspiration for a whole new product! KISSinsights, now called Qualaroo, powers on-site surveys and targeted interactions for thousands of companies.

Typically a tangent will run its course after two or three minutes and you can simply ask the next question. If not, you can simply interject to apologize and say that you want to make sure that there is time to get to the next question.

Avoiding the Wish List

Some people will evade your questions and say, "Here's what I want." They'll start listing features and options; I've even had people start sketching mockups in coffee shop meetings!

On the surface, this sounds amazing: a prospective customer practically writing your product requirements for you. The truth is different: thousands of failed products are created based on what customers *said* they wanted. You've probably worked on at least one of them in the past.*

You don't need to learn what customers say they *want*; you need to learn how customers *behave* and what they *need*. In other words, focus on their problem, not their suggested solution.

Away from Features—Back to the Problem

As soon as a person starts talking about feature ideas or specific solutions, quickly redirect the conversation. This takes some delicacy because you don't want to imply that her ideas aren't good. Her feature ideas may actually be great; they're just not what you need right now. The most common transition I use is to ask how a requested feature or sketch would solve her problems:

> *You're saying that you'd like [feature]? Could you walk me through when and how you would use it?*
>
> *[Listen to her answer, then transition from feature to back to problem]*
>
> *So, it sounds like today you have the problem of _____. Is that accurate? Can you tell me more about this problem? I want to be sure I fully understand it so we can work on solving it.*

The problem of interviewees suggesting features is even more of a challenge if you have an existing product and customers. People who have already paid you money or signed a contract feel that they have earned the right to make feature requests. (If they've paid enough money, they also expect you to tell them how long it will be until that feature is built and released.)

---

* There's a terrific episode of *The Simpsons* that illustrates this point. Homer discovers he has a long-lost half-brother, Herb, who owns the fictional Powell Motors company. When Herb encourages Homer to design a car for the average American consumer, Homer includes shag carpeting, an isolation bubble for the kids, and three horns that play "La Cucaracha" when honked. Naturally, no one actually wants to buy a car like that, and Powell Motors goes out of business (*http://simpsons.wikia.com/wiki/The_Homer*).

Entertainingly, a team actually built the Homer for the 24 Hours of LeMons race (*http://techland.time.com/2013/06/27/finally-homer-simpson-designed-car-the-homer-comes-to-life*).

Business innovators often cite the alleged Henry Ford quote, *"If I had asked my customers what they wanted, they would have said a faster horse."** You can imagine the customer development interview that might have occurred back then:

> **Customer:** *I need a faster horse. When are you going to build one?*

> **Interviewer:** *I want to make sure that whatever we build truly solves your problem. Can you tell me, if you had a faster horse right now, how would that make your life easier?*

> **Customer:** *I'd be able to get to work faster, of course!*

The Magic Wand Question

What customers ask for is constrained by what they already know and is often not the best solution. They may even feel embarrassed to mention ideas that they don't fully understand. That's an incredibly limiting perspective. *The question that helps open their minds is the magic wand question:*

> *If you could wave a magic wand and change anything—doesn't matter if it's possible or not—about [problem area], what would it be?*

It's a little bit silly, and that's deliberate. The mention of a magic wand is unexpected in a conversation between adults—it makes people smile and loosen up. Magic wands don't know about regulations or org charts or technology limitations—they just get the job done. In a consumer context, magic wands address more basic human constraints. Like fairy godmothers, magic wands are not limited by time or money.

By freeing people up, the magic wand question allows people to talk about larger, more complicated pain points. (It's not uncommon for a prospective customer to ask for something impossible that isn't at all.) That adds up to more attractive problems for you to solve.

Get in the habit of asking this question. You'll use it a lot. People are wired to make suggestions and ask for specific solutions, not to describe their problems. This style of questioning won't result in a customer inventing the Model T, but it will shift him to thinking in terms of the underlying problem.

---

* There's no evidence that Henry Ford ever said this, though many people, including his own great-grandson, have attributed it to him. See *http://quoteinvestigator.com/2011/07/28/ford-faster-horse/*.

Once you've asked the magic wand question, you can explain a little bit about what you're trying to do:

In the past, we've worked on products that were supposed to do something specific, but they didn't solve the real problem. We're trying to avoid that and make sure we build something that will help with your situation and address the things that make your life harder.

That's a message that almost any customer will understand—we've all bought products that didn't deliver what they promised.

Avoiding Product Specifics

What if the interviewee starts asking specific questions about your product? Especially if she is highly motivated to solve this problem, she will be eager to see what you're building.

You may or may not have a product in progress, but in any case, it's best not to show the interviewee your product or talk about specifics until the very end of your conversation. Better yet, schedule a separate interview for talking about solutions.

Why is it a bad idea to show your product at this stage? The reason is that images or tangible specs will taint everything that your interviewee was going to say. Instead of thinking about how she works and her frustrations, she will subconsciously tailor her answers based on your product. (This is a variation on the "If you have a hammer, everything looks like a nail" principle.)*

If an interviewee is eager to see your product or visuals first, you can explain that you'd like to hear about her experiences and frustrations first so that she's not influenced by what already exists. You can always offer to schedule a follow-up demo in the future, but once you've shown something, you'll never be able to go back and get pure feedback from this person.

If you don't have anything to show yet, it's OK to say so. You can say something like "We are hoping to solve the problem of people managing their personal finances, and in order to do that really well we need to first understand exactly what people are doing today and where they are struggling."

---

* This concept was popularized by Abraham Maslow, who wrote in *The Psychology of Science*, "I suppose it is tempting, if the only tool you have is a hammer, to treat everything as if it were a nail." I prefer the earlier usage by another Abraham. Abraham Kaplan said, "Give a small boy a hammer, and he will find that everything he encounters requires pounding" (*https://en.wikipedia.org/wiki/Law_of_the_instrument*).

Going Long

You asked for 20 minutes of a person's time, but sometimes you'll find that he is still talking enthusiastically past that time. (That's why I don't recommend scheduling back-to-back conversations every half-hour.) Even if your interviewee seems eager to continue talking, he may have lost track of time. You don't want to inconvenience him by inadvertently making him late to his next commitment. If you near the 30-minute mark and he is still talking, it's a good idea to gently interrupt with "Excuse me—I'd love to continue the conversation, but I don't want to take up too much of your time."

I don't recommend extending interviews much beyond the 45-minute mark, no matter how enthusiastic you both are. You'll get diminishing returns and risk using up that person's goodwill. A better approach is to request permission to contact him with follow-up questions.

It is tempting to try and cram as much as possible into your initial conversation. What if this is the only opportunity you get to talk to him? It's counterintuitive, but doing one favor for you actually primes people to do a second one. Have you ever been asked for a small charitable donation, and then been hit up for a larger one later? That's the foot-in-the-door technique, and it's much more effective than asking you for the big bucks in the first interaction.*

Offer to schedule a second interview once you've learned more or have some early sketches to show. Remember, some of the target customers you interview early on are likely to become your future evangelists—even if what you end up building is completely different from where you started.

The Last Few Minutes

Just as the first minute is critical to get someone talking, the last minute is critical to building a relationship with her. You don't want the interviewee to regret having given you the last 20 to 30 minutes of her time.

---

* The Wikipedia article on the topic describes the foot-in-the-door technique this way: "When someone expresses support for an idea or concept, that person is more likely to then remain consistent with their prior expression of support by committing to it in a more concrete fashion" (http://en.wikipedia.org/wiki/Foot-in-the-door_technique).

The most often cited examples of foot-in-the-door research date from social psychology experiments done in the 1960s. A more recent meta-analysis of foot-in-the-door tactics (http://psp.sagepub.com/content/9/2/181) questions the strength of the phenomenon.

Nonetheless, I've seen it work. If your prospective customers aren't responding to your follow-up emails, I'd hesitate to blame social psychology and take that as a cue that the problem you're solving is not compelling enough to warrant further attention.

It's your job, in the last few minutes of your conversation, to do three things:

- Offer some of your own time to the interviewee
- Make the interviewee feel that she succeeded in helping you
- Thank her personally for giving her time

Whatever you say, it must be personal and genuine. This isn't the conclusion of a business transaction; it's the end of a conversation with someone you probably want to talk to again in the future. Here's what I say, but make sure what you say works with your personal speaking style:

> *[Name], I think you've answered all the questions I had. Is there anything I can answer for you?*
>
> *[Pause, answer questions as needed]*
>
> *Thank you so much for talking with me today. It was really helpful for me to hear you talk about [repeat a problem or situation the interviewee discussed]. That's the type of detail that it's just impossible for me to learn without talking to real people who are experiencing it.*
>
> *Can I keep you in the loop as I continue to learn more? If I have further questions, or once I'm closer to building an actual solution, can I get back in touch with you?*
>
> *[Pause]*
>
> *Thanks again, and have a good rest of your day!*

This is another application of the foot-in-the-door technique. By asking people if you can contact them again, you're reinforcing their role as the expert. You're asking them for a favor, but it feels like a compliment.

I frequently come back with follow-up questions, either later in the process when I think I've spotted a pattern and need some more data points, or once I have a minimum viable product to show the customer.

Customer? What Customer?

You may have noticed that I've avoided using the word customer in my dialogues with the interviewee. When I'm talking with someone, I never call her a customer or refer to other customers. Seems a little odd for a book on customer development, right?

There's a reason for this: I don't want the person on the other side of the table to think of herself as a customer (yet) because that puts her in a negotiating mind-set. Have you ever negotiated to get a better price on something? It's generally considered disadvantageous to show enthusiasm or reveal too much: if the salesperson knows you need something, he's less likely to offer a price break. When people negotiate, they try to say as little as possible. That's the last thing you want from your interviewees!

Even when you state that you don't have a product and you're not trying to sell something, calling someone a customer can put her in that tacit, negotiating mind-set. Talking about "you" or "a person" or "some people" preserves the feeling of an open conversation.

After the Interview

The process of interviewing should be every bit as iterative as the process of building your product. In other words, you won't get it right the first time. You'll need to keep assessing what you did and how well it worked, and fine-tuning the areas that didn't work as well as you would have liked.

While the interview is still fresh in your mind, take five minutes to ask yourself or your note-taker the following questions:

- Did the opening minute of the interview go smoothly? Did the interviewee start talking right away?

- Did I unintentionally ask leading questions or offer an opinion that may have biased what the interviewee said? (You probably won't notice if you did this. If you worked with a note-taker, he is more likely to have caught these slip-ups.)

- Did any of my questions lead to very short or bland answers? Is there a way I could revise them to be more open-ended and effective?

- Did I ask any questions on the fly, or did the interviewee bring up any questions or ideas that I should add to my interview template?

- Was there anything that I wish I had learned but we just didn't get there? How could I get at that information next time?

- Where did the interviewee show the most emotion? Which questions prompted the most detailed and enthusiastic replies?

If you don't run through this checklist immediately after the interview, you will forget a lot of vivid detail. You'll always have your notes, but that subjective feeling of what went well and poorly fades quickly.

This is also a good time to focus on the subjective qualities of your conversation. What was the dominant emotion this person expressed? Anger, giddiness, frustration, shame, curiosity, excitement? If you had to summarize the tone of the conversation in one sentence to a friend, what would it be? I'll focus more on analyzing your notes in Chapter 6, but this isn't about analysis—it's about your gut feeling. Jot it down now before it fades away.

Take some time before your next scheduled interview to adjust the areas that need improvement. Then start the process all over again!

What if the Interviews Aren't Going Well?

I hesitated to write this section because the last thing I want is for readers to think that customer development interviews are something you have to do perfectly to get results. The vast majority of the time, your interviews will go just fine. You'll make some mistakes, but your interviewees will be forgiving or, most likely, won't even notice.

Nonetheless I want to share some troubleshooting tips, on the slight chance that you find yourself in one of these awkward situations. I've done enough customer development interviews that both of these things have happened to me at some point:

My interviewees sound annoyed

> Even if you have scheduled time to talk, I recommend starting your interview by confirming that this is still a good time. It doesn't happen often, but occasionally the person on the other end of the phone is busy or just having a bad day and I've rescheduled the conversation.

If that's not the issue, the most likely culprit behind impatience or annoyance is a conflict in expectations. This is why I gave examples of introductory emails in Chapter 3. Is it possible that your interviewee expected a shorter call, an existing product, or compensation for his time? When that happens, it will be a bad experience for him and is less likely to be useful for you.

I feel like I'm insulting my interviewees

Sometimes when you probe into a prospective customer's pain points, the customer interprets your comments as critical or judging. This typically means that you need to use softening language. Pausing, or adding phrases like "may I ask" or "let me clarify" before asking a probing question can prepare the interviewee to dig deeper. Individual words—like *some*, *slight*, *minor*, or *occasional*—can help. (For more detail, refer back to "Be Diplomatic with 'Why?'".)

If you feel the interviewee closing up versus opening up, phrases that build empathy can be helpful. Using "we've experienced..." or "other people have told me that..." are good phrases that reassure the interviewee.

Get Out (Now!)

Now it's time to stop reading. Put the book down and go talk to a customer.

We've covered the questions to ask, the techniques for getting people to talk, and the prompts that keep them talking. The only missing ingredient is you taking action. I'm watching you: don't start reading Chapter 6 until you've done at least two interviews. Get out of the building!

Key Takeaways

- Do a practice interview with a colleague.

- Do pair interviewing to improve your interviews and involve more people in customer development (including those who may not be comfortable talking directly with customers).

- Keep your tone conversational and personal.

- After you ask your first question, wait a full minute before asking a follow-up question.

- Listen for emotion when taking notes. Emotion is prioritization.

- Listen for anything that validates or invalidates your hypothesis and for anything that takes you by surprise.

- Listen when customers go on tangents. If a tangent recurs, it might be a different opportunity to explore.

- When customers suggest features or solutions, guide them back to talking about the problem.

- Review your notes immediately after interviews to improve your interviews and recap what was said.

CHAPTER 6

What Does a Validated Hypothesis Look Like?

At first people would tell me, "That's a good idea," and I would get excited. But after doing a few interviews, I would see some people have an a-ha moment and start talking and talking excitedly. The more interviews I did, the more I felt I could tell the difference between people who were trying to be nice and people who really had a problem that I could solve.

—Bartosz Malutko, Starters CEO

Now that you've started doing customer development interviews, you're probably impatiently awaiting some answers. You created focused and falsifiable hypotheses, you found people to talk to, and you were disciplined in asking open-ended questions and letting the customer be the expert. Now is the time to start taking what you've learned and using it to guide your decisions.

In this chapter, we'll talk through how to get reliable answers from your interview responses. You'll learn why you should be a temporary pessimist, when to distrust what you're hearing, and how to reduce bias. We'll also cover:

- Sharing the story with your team

- How many interviews you need

- What you should be learning after 2, 5, and 10 interviews

- What to do if your interviews aren't going well
- How to recognize a validated hypothesis

What does validating a hypothesis mean? Does it mean you have a guaranteed product success? Does it mean that you cannot build anything until you've completed enough interviews? Does it mean that you can stop doing customer development now?

No, no, and no.

Validation simply means that you're confident enough to continue investing time and effort in this direction. It also doesn't mean that you need to wait until you've completed 10, 15, or 20 interviews before writing a line of code! Customer development happens in parallel with product development, which means that you may be starting to create an MVP at any point in your interview timeline. It also means that you should be continuing to talk to customers even after you've started building your product or service.

Maintaining a Healthy Skepticism

Customer development interviews are subjective, and that's a challenge: it's easy to hear what you want to hear. Without even meaning to, most people focus on the positives. We hear the word *maybe*, we see a smile, and we ignore the hesitation or tense body language.

It's all too easy to interpret responses to prove your hypotheses right even if they aren't. *If you do that, you've wasted a ton of time.* Let's avoid that fate.

Are They Telling You What You Want to Hear?

What will you hear when people are too eager to please? There's often a difference between politeness and honesty. You have to learn to read between the lines, and the subtext of the conversation can be slightly different depending on whether your product is aimed at consumers or at businesses.

Generally speaking, consumers don't want to disappoint you. If you've done a good job in building rapport and sounding human, your interviewee wants to cooperate and make you happy. She may say that she's experiencing a problem or behaving in a certain way even though it's not true. She may say that she would pay for a solution that allowed her to accomplish something, but in reality she would never hand over her credit card.

For those of you who work with enterprise products, this takes on a different tone. Your interviewee may feel that being professional means valuing politeness over honesty. He may think he is being diplomatic by agreeing that something is possible when he knows it's highly improbable.

He may also believe that these conversations are an invitation to verbal horse-trading: by agreeing with you in one area, he may feel that he has earned the right to ask for something that he wants later.

In both of these situations, you may hear responses that align a little too perfectly with what you were hoping to hear. When you hear an interviewee say something that confirms your assumptions, don't stop there. Be skeptical.

I often say, *"If someone says maybe, write it down as no."*

Is the Customer Saying Something Real or Aspirational?

It's not enough for someone to say that she wants something—a product, a service, the ability to accomplish a task. It's free and easy to want.

Actually changing behaviors, spending money, or learning something new has a cost. You need to figure out the difference between want and will, and uncovering that difference requires discipline in how you talk to your target customers. If you ask a question and the person says "yes," that carries significantly less weight than if he brought up the subject unprompted.

In Chapter 4, I talked about the importance of asking open-ended questions. It's almost always better to avoid yes-or-no questions entirely, but in the beginning that's a hard habit to form. You'll slip up occasionally and ask something like "Would you do X?" or "Would you like X?" That's fine, as long as you recognize that you can't take the customer's response at face value. You need to challenge it.

Years ago, I worked with a large bank on some in-person customer research. An executive with the bank insisted on asking the question "Are you concerned with the security of your financial information?" I pointed out that no one would ever say "no" to that question, but to no avail. As I predicted, 10 of the 10 people I spoke with answered that, of course, they were very concerned with the security and privacy of their financial information. As one of them was leaving, I thanked him and said, "In order to get your $50 gratuity, I'll need you to write down your mother's maiden name and social security number." Without hesitation, the man grabbed a ballpoint pen and reached for my sheet of paper. I stopped him before he could write anything, but my point was made. Very concerned about security... until $50 was on the line.

A better way to phrase that initial question would have been to ask about existing behavior, such as *"What actions do you believe people can take to keep their financial information secure?"* If you've already asked a yes-or-no question and gotten a "yes," you'll want to use a more open-ended question in subsequent interviews.

A reliable answer should include some tangible actions, such as "choose secure passwords" or "always log out after using a bank website." In contrast, consider a response like "I don't know" or "I always read about someone hacking into somewhere and getting credit card numbers, but there's really nothing you can do to stop that."

Even if you've phrased your questions well, sometimes customers will sound extremely enthusiastic even though they're unlikely to buy or use your product. I experienced this firsthand when I ran design and research for a personal finance product. When I did customer interviews to select people for our beta program, almost everyone was passionate about problems with managing their money. They described their frustrations in detail. When they saw a demo, they loved the idea of the product. Most said that they would definitely use such a product, even pay for it. And yet somehow, we didn't end up with anything approaching 100% usage. (You're shocked, I know.)

Over time, I began to see differences in the specific words people used. The people who became customers used a more active voice and described specifics; others used a more passive voice and talked in hypothetical terms. If you've taken verbatim notes, look for patterns like those in Table 6-1.

Table 6-1. Comparing real and aspirational speech patterns

People who became customers said	Noncustomers said
I've already tried… Here's how I do…	Plan on doing… Haven't tried yet… Keep meaning to…
I need to be able to do [task] faster/better because… Here are the things making it difficult for me to do [task] currently…	[Task] is impossible… I just don't know how anyone does [task]…
This would help me achieve [goal]… If I had this, here's what I could do…	I wish I had… It'd be interesting to see… Well, once I had it, I'd be able to figure out how to use it…
Right now…	Soon… As soon as [some event happens]… Almost ready to…
Here's how I do…	I don't! I really should do…

It turned out I was hearing from a lot of people who were smiling and passionate and talking about what they *wished* they would do. Managing your finances well is one of those goals, like losing 10 pounds or flossing daily, which everyone feels they *ought* to do.

The best predictor of future behavior is current behavior. Focusing on specific examples of current behavior is the best way to defuse aspirational speak. If an interviewee talks about wanting to lose 10 pounds, ask what exercise she's done in the past week. If someone talks about wanting to streamline the project management process, ask which meetings or bottlenecks she's eliminated so far.

If your interview notes contain lots of exclamation points but little real-world behavioral evidence, you're not validating your hypothesis. We'll talk more about validating (or invalidating) your hypothesis later in this chapter. Remember that the most important thing is to do one or the other *quickly*. If your hypothesis is invalid, the sooner you know that, the sooner you can adjust it and make progress. If you validate your hypothesis quickly, you can get on with building an MVP (which I'll cover in more detail in Chapter 7).

But before we get too far ahead of ourselves, let's talk about your notes, which will help you in validating or invalidating your hypothesis.

Keeping Organized Notes

When I was at KISSmetrics, consolidating customer development insights across the team was one of my highest priorities. I averaged 10–15 customer interviews per week (and some weeks, *many* more). The founders typically had as many conversations (though rarely as structured) with customers. As the team grew, customer support and sales engineering also talked with customers daily. That's a lot of notes to keep straight!

Keeping track of that much information is tricky enough with just one person. And ideally, many if not all of the people building products on your team are participating in customer development.

I quickly learned that if you've taken enough notes to accurately capture what someone said in a 20-minute interview, you've got more words than you can effectively share with your team. It's impossible for every person to read every word of customer development notes. Having some structure around summarizing and maintaining notes is critical.

Keeping Your Notes in One File

For projects where I am the primary interviewer, I keep a single Word document with all of the notes from all customer interviews. Right before I talk to a new person, I add a few blank lines, type in the person's name and company in bold, and copy and paste my simple interview template (which was presented in Chapter 5).

If you have multiple people interviewing, Google Docs is a better choice because it supports co-editing. You won't need to worry about accidentally overwriting each other's notes if two or more people are conducting interviews at the same time.

Having all of your notes in a single document makes it easier to search later on. If you remember that someone previously mentioned "email integration," you could search for that phrase instead of having to remember who said it. It's also easy to see the number of times a specific word or product name was used. You can do this across multiple documents, but it's much slower.

Some people I've worked with recommend Evernote for customer development. One advantage of Evernote is its availability across multiple platforms. If you think of something later, you can look it up on your phone or iPad and make a quick note about it. But personally, I use Word or Google Docs.

Creating a Summary

I use a second Word document when creating summaries. Using a separate document for summaries makes it easier to skim and look for patterns. This document is lightweight enough that I can share it with my team without burying them in information.

The first step is to summarize what you learned from each interview. But don't stop there. You shouldn't be simply shortening what the interviewee told you, but drawing some conclusions and recommended next steps. Customer development is only effective if it drives your team to focus and avoid spending time on ineffective activities.

If the customer disagrees with the team's beliefs, a summary document probably won't be enough to convince people to change their minds. This is why I emphasized the practice of pair interviewing in Chapter 5. A team member who has participated in a few interviews, even if only as a note-taker, will be more receptive to summarized feedback. Pull out the full version of your notes for people who need more proof of what customers are saying, and see if you can persuade some of those folks to act as note-takers in future interviews.

As you remember from Chapter 5, the most important areas to capture in note-taking are:

- Something that validates your hypotheses
- Something that invalidates your hypotheses

- Anything that takes you by surprise

- Anything full of emotion

Those areas are where most of your learning will happen. When I'm summarizing, I force myself to boil each interview down to five to seven bullet points containing the most *interesting* information. This makes me prioritize what I heard and pick out the most valuable things I learned from each interview.

When you have multiple interviewers, each person can prioritize her own notes into a total of five to seven bullets for three sections: Validates, Invalidates, and Also Interesting.

If you're not sure how to prioritize, let the interviewee's emotion be the deciding factor. A matter-of-fact statement that supports one of your assumptions is interesting, but not nearly as interesting as an enthusiastic five-minute tangent on a competitor's product.

Here's a five-point summary from a KISSmetrics interview:

Joanne, marketing director, midsized company

Validates

"I use Google Analytics but it leaves me with more questions than it answers, honestly." (We assumed that our customers already use Google Analytics but have outgrown it.)

Analytics is a lower priority because developers are working on product features, so she feels like she's working in the dark. (As we thought, setting up the product only happens if it requires minimal developer resources.)

Invalidates

No online marketing efforts at all! "Knowing where people came from before they got to my site—well, it doesn't affect me, right? So I'm not sure why I'd need to know." (We'd assumed that market attribution was critical to our customers—*this invalidates that assumption!*)

Also interesting

Long tangent on customer support—others in the company don't see some of the product problems because they don't have access to support emails that make the problem obvious.

Interested in early beta access; willing to pay a developer to help with install.

Rallying the Team Around New Information

The best way to ensure that your customer development efforts improve your product development efforts is to maximize the number of people on your team who talk to customers. Those people will organically bring that customer knowledge into their day-to-day decisions around product scope, implementation details, design details, and marketing.

Pair interviewing is one valuable technique for bringing more people into the customer's world. Another technique is to invite a large group of people to help categorize customer feedback. At Yammer, we typically do this using sticky notes in a large physical space. This requires retranscribing feedback, which takes extra time. However, the act of moving around physical sticky notes encourages people to discuss and react to the feedback and helps it to sink in more effectively (Figure 6-1).

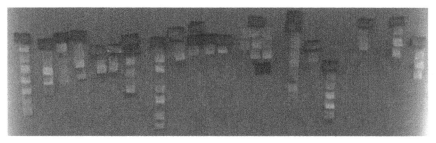

Figure 6-1. Invite the whole team to help categorize customer comments, and they'll pay more attention to what you're learning

Minds don't change immediately, though. Even when someone sees her assumptions invalidated firsthand, it takes time and repetition to turn that new information into a course correction.

Your job is to help your team to see the world through the eyes of the customer and make the necessary changes to stay focused and avoid wasted effort. Here are some tips to help you share what you're learning effectively:

Sell what you're learning

What you're learning is critical. You're telling a story that may save or doom your product. It's critical that you realize how important these insights are and frame them as such. Don't send out an email with a boring subject line like "Customer interview summaries" unless you want people to tune you out.

They lack context: supply it

One of the biggest challenges in reporting back to your team is remembering that *they lack context*. Once you've heard multiple customers share how they behave and what they believe, it's hard to remember *not* understanding their situations. This isn't unique to customer development; it goes back to the curse of knowledge mentioned in Chapter 5. The curse of knowledge blinds you to the realization that you need to explain each step that brought you closer to a conclusion. For people who didn't participate in the conversation, it isn't immediately obvious which comments, body language, or questions are significant.

Encourage questions (don't jump to recommendations)

Encourage questions and discussion. Jumping directly to your recommendations or opinions effectively shuts your team out of the loop. If others don't feel that they're participating in the customer development process, they may start to subtly resist it. The first step to getting people to participate? Make sure they're listening.

Be where the decisions are made

Customer development insights should turn into action items and decisions. It's better to share information for five minutes during a product scope or prioritization meeting than to hold an hour-long meeting where people listen and no one takes action.

Set up a regular schedule for sharing what you've learned. How often should that be?

It depends. Use the frequency that makes sense for the size and velocity of your company. Let me tell you what worked for me in various settings.

At KISSmetrics, I typically consolidated and shared customer development feedback just before our weekly product prioritization meetings. In a typical week, I might have completed 5–10 interviews, each of which I summarized as described in the previous section.

At Yammer, those of us doing customer development post our interview notes to our internal Yammer network as soon as the interview is completed. Everyone on the project team can read the interview notes immediately and ask questions. To spread information across product teams, we also share summaries at a monthly meeting to discuss user research and analytics updates. Those meetings are more conversational, so we present lightweight slide decks with just enough information to spur a conversation (see Figure 6-2).

Insights from the 1%

- They tend to work with clients and deal with **constantly changing information**.
- They use Yammer to share and **archive** knowledge across teams.
- They value the **fast pace** of Yammer, compared to email.
- They are **logged in all day, every day**.
- They have been using Yammer **consistently** from the beginning.
- They are **managers** trying to be more effective leaders or **employees using Yammer to stand out**.
- They reported inconsistent syncing across devices as their **biggest frustration**.

Figure 6-2. Short summary slides, like this one summarizing customer development interviews with the most active customers on Yammer, encourage discussion

How Many Interviews Do You Need?

Short answer 1: It depends.

Short answer 2: 15–20.

I'm not sure that either of these short answers is really helpful, but I'd hate to have you skim the next few pages looking for a real answer. So let's start with these answers, and I'll explain more about what you'll encounter along the way.

After two interviews, look at your questions and notes and adapt your interview.

After five interviews, you should have encountered at least one excited person.

After 10 interviews, you should see patterns in the responses you're getting.

How many interviews are enough?

After enough interviews, you'll know it.* You'll no longer hear things that surprise you.

In the following sections, I'll expand on these answers.

---

* I know; this is a very frustrating and subjective answer. It reminds me of verbal driving directions in New England: go to the center of town and turn left. How will you know when you get to the center of town? Unless you've been in a small New England town, you might not believe this is enough information. Once you have, you realize that it is.

After Two Interviews: Are You Learning What You Need to Learn?

In Chapter 5, we talked about taking a few minutes after your first customer interview to figure out which elements were most successful. Most likely, the first changes you made to your interviews related to your tone and the phrasing of your questions.

Once you've completed two or three interviews, you'll have to make a more critical assessment. *Are you learning what you need to learn?*

Components of a validated hypothesis

A validated hypothesis typically has four components, expressed enthusiastically:

- The customer confirms that there is definitely a problem or pain point
- The customer believes that the problem can and should be resolved
- The customer has actively invested (effort, time, money, learning curve) in trying to solve this problem
- The customer doesn't have circumstances beyond his control that prevent him from trying to fix the problem or pain point*

What each interview should tell you

When you reread your notes from an interview, you need to feel confident that you understood the depth of this person's pain point and the level of her motivation to fix it.

You should be able to confidently answer questions like:

- If I had a product today that completely solved this customer's problem, do I see any obstacles that would prevent her from buying or using it?
- How would she use it and fit it into her day-to-day activities?
- What would it replace?
- If she would not buy my solution, what are the specific reasons why not?

---

* Even if the customer is willing to invest time and resources into solving a problem, she may be constrained by other stakeholders, by rules or regulations, or by cultural or social norms about what is acceptable.

For example, teachers may be willing to invest in a solution that allows them to more effectively educate, but be unable to override a curriculum set at the state level. Restaurant workers may wish to reduce food waste, but be constrained by health regulations. Teenagers may be desperate for a job training program but live in a place with no viable public transit and no adult able to drive them to the location.

If you can't answer these questions, modify your interview questions (see the sidebar below).

Two interviews are not enough to give you the confidence that you are correct. They are solely an indicator that you're not *completely* incorrect.

Changing Your Interview Questions

Don't worry about maintaining consistency across your interviews. When I did social psychology research as an undergraduate, it was drilled into me that I had to deliver the same script, in the same manner, to avoid introducing bias into a study. I heard similar advice when I first started doing usability testing: don't change the questions or you'll bias the results. This is *not* the case with customer development interviews. You're not studying a specific situation where all variables but one are controlled: you're learning about unique individuals in different environments who don't always make decisions rationally.

Over time, your questions and style will naturally evolve. You'll adapt what you say and how you say it based on the person you're talking to. The most important thing is to always be learning.

For these or any other concerns, the best way to troubleshoot your questions is to get a second opinion. Grab a coworker and have her read your interview request or listen to you ask your questions. Another person's perspective makes it much easier to pick up on minor points that may be misinterpreted by others.

Within Five Interviews: The First Really Excited Person

Within the first five interviews, you'll encounter at least one person who is *really* excited about your idea. At minimum, if you've identified a good problem to solve, someone will give you a direct referral ("This doesn't affect me, but I know *exactly* who you should talk to"). If you've heard something like that, great! Keep going.

If you haven't, one of the following is likely true:

- You're talking to the wrong people
- Your problem isn't really a problem

Either way, this invalidates your hypothesis (remember that the hypothesis consists of two parts: that this type of person has this type of problem).

It's possible to talk to one outlier. It's possible to talk to two outliers. It's highly unlikely to talk to five in a row. If five people aren't interested, it's probably because you've invalidated your hypothesis.

Congratulations! You've Invalidated Your Hypothesis!

It's alarming the first time you realize that one or more of your initial assumptions is wrong.

Try to think of it as a positive. Practically no one gets his market and product right on the first try, so it isn't a reflection on you or your product.

If you've been able to objectively accept that customers aren't biting, that's a good sign. It shows that you've been disciplined enough to talk without leading the witness and to listen without inserting your bias.

Now what? Well, part of the reason you asked open-ended questions is so that you could learn not only *what* but *why*.

Look at the behaviors your initial target customer described. Look at the reasons he gave for taking those actions. Your notes should provide clues about which customer may be a better fit. Look at your initial hypothesis as well. How would you change it based on what you have learned? Are there smaller assumptions that you've validated or invalidated?

Be sure to write down what you've learned, write a new hypothesis, and start again. It gets easier each time you do this.

Best of all, you did it within five interviews. That's much better than after you brought your product to market!

"But wait!" you might say. "Maybe I wasn't asking the right questions." That's unlikely. When you're talking to a person who really cares about solving her problem, her passion will shine through and she'll answer the question you *should have* asked.

Once you've heard your first really excited person, you may want to think about how quickly you can assemble an MVP. I generally recommend starting with 10 interviews, but if you can put together an MVP in less time than it would take to do 5 more interviews, why wait?

No matter how excited someone sounds about your product, the real test is whether or not he is willing to throw down money (or some other personal currency, such as his time, a pre-order, or an email address). If you can figure out a way to collect currency from a user within a couple of hours, go for it!

Within 10 Interviews: Patterns Emerge

Within 10 interviews, you're likely to have heard some repetition. This may come in the form of two or three people expressing similar frustrations, motivations, process limitations, or things they wish they could do.

Challenging the patterns

Once I've heard a concept three times, I deliberately try to challenge it in future interviews. I use the word challenge because the goal here is to test the pattern, not to assume that it will hold. It's tempting to use yes-or-no or "Do you agree?" questions on future participants. That introduces bias. Focus on asking about scenarios and past behaviors and let the interviewee naturally confirm the pattern (or not).

If the topic doesn't naturally come up, a helpful way to challenge the pattern you've seen is the "other people" method. You talk about invented "other people" and claim that they feel the opposite way or act in the opposite way of the pattern you've been hearing. For example:

Pattern

You've heard multiple people say that they research cars online *and then* visit a dealer.

Challenge

You might say the opposite: "*Other people* have told me that they prefer to visit the dealer and test drive a car *first, then* do research online. Could you tell me how you shop for cars?"

Be sure to follow up an "other people do this" statement with a question. This provokes your interviewee to pay more attention to what you've said and answer in more detail.* Whether he agrees or disagrees with your

---

* Social psychology research theorizes that questions "arouse the reader's uncertainty and motivate more intensive processing of message content than statements." See Robert E. Burnkrant and Daniel J. Howard, "Effects of the Use of Introductory Rhetorical Questions Versus Statements on Information Processing," *Journal of Personality and Social Psychology*, vol 47(6), Dec 1984.

mythical other people, he will react to the comparison by describing exactly how he is different from or similar to them.

No patterns yet?

What if you aren't hearing patterns? It is possible to talk with 10 or more people and hear a lot of responses that seem genuine and evoke emotion but don't seem to fall into a pattern. What this typically means is that you've targeted too broad a customer audience. You may be talking to multiple different types of people, all of whom are plausible customers but have different needs.

I recommend narrowing the type of people you're talking to. Try to focus in on one job title, lifestyle, technical competence, type of company, or other limiting category. This will help you to spot patterns more quickly so you can continue learning and don't get frustrated. Don't worry about aiming too narrow—your goal is to validate or invalidate as quickly as possible.

How Many Interviews Are Enough?

As I mentioned earlier, the real answer is "it depends." Remember that the aim of customer development is to reduce risk. As such, the number of interviews you need to do is inversely correlated with:

- Experience with customer development and your domain
- Complexity of your business model and number of dependencies
- Investment required to create and validate your MVP

Experience with customer development and industry

The more experience and comfort you have with customer development, the fewer interviews you need. (And this isn't because you substitute your judgment for getting out of the building and talking to people!) Your improved ability to target individuals means you'll talk to more of the right people early on. Asking better questions gets you better insights.

Similarly, familiarity with customers or your industry vertical shortens your cycle because your early hypotheses are based on current behaviors, decision-making patterns, and expressed needs. They're still unlikely to be completely right, but you'll have less trial-and-error time. When I was at Yodlee, I had been working with our users for several years prior to introducing customer development interviews. I already had quite a bit of insight into how users were handling their finances online and offline, so I was able to get away with fewer interviews before beginning to build product features.

How Do You Validate with an "Impossible-to-Reach" Market?

If you have a high degree of domain expertise, you don't need to invest time learning regulations, laws, and customs. Mark Abramson, a former president of USA Cycling, hypothesized that there was a better way to get crashed cyclists better care and back on their bicycles faster. He was quickly able to validate a problem and start building a solution. The "product" was a professional organization, Medicine of Cycling, which connects doctors, cycling teams, and athletes and hosts an annual conference.

As Abramson tells it, "A lot of the credit for Medicine of Cycling goes to my wife Anna, a doctor. She was talking to a trauma surgeon at Harvard who said, 'We get all these injured cyclists coming to the emergency room, and I think there's an opportunity to improve their pace of recovery and the quality of care that they receive.'"

When people start conducting customer development interviews, they aren't sure what questions to ask. But as the president of USA Cycling, Abramson had background knowledge and an existing network that allowed him to jump directly into some quick surveys. Abramson asked about how often athletes were getting injured, how much competition time they were missing, whether their competitive teams were offering insurance, and how much money they were spending.

Customer development at an event

Abramson brought this data to the 2010 Tour of California, where he was able to gather about 30 cycling team owners, managers, and physicians. "It became immediately clear that none of these people were talking to each other about problems of injury!" says Abramson. During that meeting, "we had quite a few a-ha moments. It was clear that we needed to get everyone together. We decided to put on a medical conference. Our conversation happened in May and we decided to hold our conference in November. To understand how crazy this was, accredited continuing medical education (CME) conferences usually take a year to plan."

Can customer development work for healthcare?

For those who are skeptical about customer development in the healthcare field, Abramson partially agrees. "Customer development hacks don't work. Getting in touch with physicians is practically impossible. Everyone is competing for their attention—pharmaceutical reps, EMR vendors, patients. They need to have a brick wall protecting them from distractions. We had zero success trying to cold-call receptionists."

Abramson's advice: "It's OK to start small." While typical CME conferences have hundreds or thousands of attendees, Medicine of Cycling started with 40. Instead of dozens of speakers, they had 10. "We invited the best people we knew through direct cycling contacts, and they helped to spread the word. We invited people that we knew were feeling the most pain from this problem—Tour of California physicians, Garmin's team physician, U.S. Olympic Committee physicians—and team doctors know other doctors."

Hypothesis validated!

Medicine of Cycling was able to validate their initial hypothesis—we can get cyclists healthy and back on their bikes faster by working together—fairly quickly. "That validation came about as a byproduct of getting all the right people together in the same room," says Abramson. Since then, the organization has relied on constant member feedback to continue to develop the product—rolling out professional memberships, publishing guidelines for common cycling injuries, and establishing standards of care. They're heading into their fourth annual conference.

Complexity of business model and number of dependencies

Even if you're a customer development and domain expert, certain business models require that you validate a greater number of assumptions. If your business has a dependency on working with suppliers, distributors, or other third parties, you'll need to speak with those people as well as your direct customers. If you are brokering a two-sided market, you'll need to listen to both sides and ensure that you're bringing value to both. This may double or triple the number of interviews you need to conduct. Because each party has its own pain points and constraints, you'll need to allow for enough conversations to let those patterns emerge for each target stakeholder.

The Chicken and Egg Problem: In a Two-Sided Market, Which Comes First?

If you're doing customer development with multiple stakeholders, should you talk to one target customer segment first, then the other? Or should you alternate?

LaunchBit, a startup that serves a two-sided market, validated its ideas through customer development. The company, an ad network for email, needed to understand the needs of both online marketers and content publishers.

CEO Elizabeth Yin explains, "It's hard to tackle a two-sided market. People say 'get one side first, then use that to get to the other side,' but that approach wasn't really possible for us."

"We first started out rounding up six publishers and two advertisers," said Yin. "The two advertisers were willing to test new ad inventory, so they were willing to use our MVP of minimal ad campaigns. The six publishers likewise were interested in testing the idea of monetizing their newsletters. So, in the beginning we had small numbers of participants from both sides using MVPs. We structured everything as an experiment. This worked for people who enjoy experimenting with new ideas. Once those early experiments went well, we were able to expand both groups. We started to get some scale, and that made our numbers look more interesting to potential customers who were less comfortable with experiments."

It's hard to predict who you should ideally interview first, so don't get too caught up in worrying about it. Jump in and start interviewing. You'll probably have a good sense after a couple of interviews about how it is most possible and practical to hear from all the stakeholders you are serving.

LaunchBit was able to identify painful problems for each side. Marketers didn't want to have to do one-off business development deals to advertise in newsletters. LaunchBit would give the marketers the ability to target multiple newsletters with one buy, and that won their business. Content publishers didn't want to run banner ads, even if they made money, because of concern they'd alienate readers. LaunchBit switched its ad format to text ads to keep publishers happy—and without publishers, they'd have no product for marketers.

> "Understanding the mind-set of both [publishers and marketers] is so important," says Yin. "It's really important to keep a constant pulse on what your customers are thinking. We continue to iterate based on conversations with publishers and marketers in order to meet their needs."

Investment required to create your MVP

In the Preface, I mentioned that I spent a month doing customer development interviews for KISSmetrics. In that time, I did about 50 interviews, which is probably near the high end of the spectrum. Let me explain why we needed that many interviews to support our MVP.

Technically, the beta version of KISSmetrics that came out of those 50 interviews was not the first step toward customer validation. We already had a prelaunch site where hundreds of customers had signed up and provided information about themselves and their companies. What we needed to validate was not their interest but that our approach to web analytics would be effective and differentiated for customers.

In that specific situation—a data-driven product where every customer's experience would be different and accuracy was critical—we needed to invest significant engineering resources to build something that would allow us to learn. By stacking 50 customer development interviews up-front, we were able to minimize that investment as much as possible.

In general, though, if you find yourself thinking that you will need a month or more to work on your MVP, you are probably vastly overengineering. It's worth seeking advice from a mentor who can sanity-check your idea of an MVP.

After Enough Interviews You Stop Hearing Things That Surprise You

The best indicator that you're done is that you stop hearing people say things that surprise you. You'll feel confident that you've gotten good enough insights on your customers' common problems, motivations, frustrations, and stakeholders.

Typically, it has taken me 15–20 interviews to feel confident that the problem and solution have potential. Between recruiting participants, preparing questions, taking notes, and summarizing, that equates to about two weeks of work. That may sound like a lot of effort, but if you learn that you can cut a single feature, you've already justified the investment in customer development.

This process can and should happen in parallel with developing your MVP.

One of my recent customer development projects involved learning about Yammer and how our customers are measuring success with it.

We knew that many customers were reporting on Yammer usage and successes to their bosses. (Any employee can start a free Yammer internal social media network for their company without top-down permission. As a result, there is often internal selling by advocates of Yammer to executives who need to learn more about its value.) They expressed frustration with our existing reporting tool, which we built based on "what customers asked for" as opposed to controlled research into their needs and behaviors. Before we committed to building more functionality, I wanted to make sure that we fully understood their problems so that we could provide a more effective solution.

Over a two-week period, I conducted 22 short customer interviews. By the last few interviews, I wasn't hearing any comments that were both new and significant. I could confidently make some assertions:

- How our customers put together reporting slide decks
- Which stakeholders they needed to please
- What frustrations they were encountering
- The root problems that explained *why* they were requesting certain product changes

Based on that information, I was able to identify that a couple of requests were tied to genuine pain points and recommend not building the others. More importantly, I was able to summarize what I'd learned from the interviews and share that back with our customers. This was an extra step that is particularly helpful with existing customers. Closing that loop—showing that we had taken their concerns seriously, identified their problems, and pointing to the changes we had implemented in response—strengthened our relationship with those customers.*

---

* To be fair, customers would still prefer it if you said, "Yes, of course we'll build what you asked for." But they're fairly well placated by hearing that we talked to customers, put a lot of thought into their problems, and have made progress toward fixing them—even if it's not in the manner the customer expected.

What Does a Validated Hypothesis Look Like?

And now: what you've all been waiting for—what does a validated hypothesis look like?

As an example, I'll walk through how KISSmetrics decided to build a second product, KISSinsights, based on what we learned from customers. Like most real-world stories, it's messier than pure theory.

I didn't begin by creating a problem hypothesis because I didn't realize that the problem existed until after I started talking to customers!

I didn't set out to find a new product idea. I was conducting customer development interviews for the KISSmetrics web analytics product, and the problem that ended up becoming KISSinsights emerged as a pattern I couldn't ignore.

I asked, keeping my language deliberately vague, what tools people were using for metrics for their websites. Nearly every potential customer mentioned two tools: Google Analytics and UserVoice. Many others had done usability testing, either by outsourcing it or using UserTesting.com or similar online tools to conduct usability testing in-house.

Originally, the purpose of my interviews was to validate that people needed better analytics—that they'd be willing to fire the free Google Analytics tool and instead pay to use KISSmetrics.

We weren't competing with qualitative feedback platforms or usability testing. This was a tangent—a distraction from what I was trying to learn about our web analytics product—but it was an *interesting* tangent.

When customers keep telling you something, you'd be crazy to ignore them.

After four or five interviews, I was already seeing a pattern. People were getting frustrated when they talked about getting feedback and understanding users. They felt helpless. I heard:

> *I wish I knew what people were thinking when they're on my site.*

> *I tried surveys but they were a waste of time—takes forever to write one, and then you get, like, two responses.*

> *All I hear from that feedback tab is "you're awesome" and "you suck," and neither of those is helpful.*

> *I wish I could sit on a customer's shoulder and, at the exact right moment, ask "why aren't you buying?" or "what is confusing you right now?"*

After the fourth or fifth unprompted comment, I formed a simple hypothesis:

Product manager types of people have a problem doing fast/effective/frequent customer research.

To learn more, the KISSmetrics team did two things in parallel:

- The developers created an MVP to validate customer demand—a splash page summarizing the concept leading to a survey form where customers could sign up to use the beta product when it was available.

- I began conducting customer interviews specific to this qualitative research concept. I asked what people were learning from qualitative feedback forms. I asked about other types of usability testing or research they'd done. I asked what was stopping them from doing more research. I asked what, if they could wave a magic wand and know anything about their visitors, they'd like to know.

Because we had an existing base of customers, I was able to quickly recruit and conduct 20 interviews. Within 20 interviews, I had a summary that looked like this:

What are customers doing right now to solve this problem?

Going without customer research.

What are other tools not providing/solving that customers really want?

Nonpublic feedback, ability to target people on specific pages or in the midst of specific actions.

Who is involved in collecting customer feedback today?

The product manager, who is eager to get this information. The developer, who is reluctant to take away time from coding features to spend time on this.

How severe/frequent is the pain?

Constant—"Whenever we make decisions on what to build." No visibility into *why* things aren't working.

What else did people have strong emotions around?

Hate writing surveys, hate having to ask a developer for help, embarrassed that they don't know where to start.

This made us confident enough to invest in building a very quick MVP that was poorly stylized and hard-coded to work only on the KISSmetrics site. As soon as our existing customers saw it, they started emailing us to ask, "How can I get that survey thing for my site?"

What felt like a tangent turned into an entirely new product: KISSinsights. Instead of a persistent and generic feedback tab, the KISSinsights survey could be configured to pop up only to visitors who'd been on a page for a certain amount of time and show a highly relevant, specific question. Best yet, we could provide prewritten survey questions so that people didn't have to write their own.

Instead of the typical 1% to 2% response rates on surveys, KISSinsights customers were seeing anywhere from 10% to 40% response rates with high-signal, actionable responses. One customer, OfficeDrop, used KISSinsights to identify issues that led to a 40% increase in their signup conversion rate.* In 2012, the KISSinsights product was sold to another company and rebranded as Qualaroo. Qualaroo continues to use customer development to evolve the product and business model.

Now What?

There's a natural ebb and flow to customer development. Once you've validated a hypothesis, the next step is to move forward in that direction.

If you don't have a product yet, you'll need to take what you've learned and use it in building (or changing) your MVP. In Chapter 7, we'll cover different types of MVPs so that you can figure out which best maps to the resources you have and the questions you need to answer.

If you're working with an existing product and looking for ways to improve it, Chapter 8 will feel like more familiar territory to you. Still, I encourage you to read Chapter 7—you may be surprised by how well MVPs have worked for even the largest companies.

---

* *http://blog.kissmetrics.com/1-2-punch-for-increasing-conversion/*

Key Takeaways

- Be skeptical about validating your hypothesis.

- Listen for clues that the customer has tried to solve the problem; many people think they *should* solve a problem, but won't really buy your product.

- The best predictor of future behavior is current behavior. Lots of exclamation points but little real-world evidence does not validate your hypothesis.

- Create a summary document in which you reduce each interview to about five bullet points, grouping them under Validates, Invalidates, and Also Interesting.

- A validated hypothesis includes the customer confirming the problem, believing it can be resolved, having tried to resolve it, and not having anything from blocking him from trying to fix it.

- Within five interviews you should meet a really excited person; if you don't, you've invalidated your hypothesis.

- Within 10 interviews, you'll start seeing patterns. Challenge patterns by talking about mythical "other people" who do something else in your next interview, and asking the interviewee to state whether he behaves like the other people or like the pattern you've identified.

- You've done enough interviews when you stop hearing things that surprise you.

CHAPTER 7

What Kind of Minimum Viable Product Should I Build?

You're not going to discover the truth by talking—you'll find it by doing. So stop worrying about the ideal set of product features and make your best guess with the information you have and get an MVP—however you define it—into the hands of customers. It's the only way to keep the discovery process going.

—Kevin Dewalt, CEO of soHelpful.me and former Entrepreneur-in-Residence for the National Science Foundation

So I asked, "Would it be cheaper to rent a camera and plane or helicopter and fly over the farmer's field, hand-process the data, and see if that's the information farmers would pay for? Couldn't you do that in a day or two, for a tenth of the money you're looking for?" They thought about it for a while and laughed and said, "We're engineers and we wanted to test all the cool technology, but you want us to test whether we first have a product that customers care about and whether it's a business. We can do that."

—Steve Blank

So far in this book, we've focused on validating your initial hypotheses and assumptions, rather than validating the solutions that come next, the minimum viable product (MVP) that you will build.

I've done this deliberately because many companies are so eager to start building their MVP that they miss multiple opportunities to reduce risk and identify mistakes. It's far faster and cheaper to catch your errors while you're still in the thinking stage. Once you've built a prototype or product, correcting errors in your thinking is far more expensive.

However, the only proof that customers will pay for your product comes *when customers pay for your product.**

In this chapter, I'll walk through how to think about your MVP. I'll also cover:

- Setting the right goal for your MVP

- Types of MVPs

- Use cases for different types of MVPs

--- **NOTE** ---

If you have existing products and customers, read Chapter 8, which includes common objections to MVPs and addresses the dynamics you may face in dealing with internal teams as well as with partners and customers.

What Should My MVP Do for Me?

The goal of an MVP is to maximize learning while minimizing risk and investment.

Your aim should be to validate your hypotheses and assumptions, and no more. Your MVP does not need to be perfect looking, fully featured, scalable, or even involve code.

In fact, it doesn't need to be a version of your product at all! A common mistake I've heard entrepreneurs make is to say, "OK, let's start with our final product and figure out what features to cut so we can quickly ship an MVP." That's the wrong mind-set—assuming that you already know what the "final" product should look like before it makes first contact with customers.

More importantly, that approach assumes that your greatest risk relates to product functionality. For many prospective companies, the biggest risks are less likely to be around product functionality and more likely around

---

* Paying for the product doesn't necessarily mean cash in hand; it may be giving you a credit card number, a purchase order, or an investment of time in learning your technology or process.

distribution, aligning pricing with value, and ability to work with resources and partners. The most important question that your MVP can answer may be something like:

- Can we get this product in front of the right customers?
- Are customers willing to pay for the value that this product promises?
- How does the customer measure the value she gets from the product?
- What pricing model aligns with customer value and the customer's ability to pay?

Understanding which questions you need to answer first will help you to craft the most relevant MVP.

MVP Types

There is no strict definition of what comprises an MVP—at least not in terms of how many features to include or what type of technology to use.

MVPs are a means of validating your biggest assumptions and minimizing your biggest risks, and those will be different for every company and product. Sometimes (as you'll see later in this chapter) they aren't even real products at all.

Minimum means that you are focusing on how to learn with the smallest investment of time and resources. If you find yourself planning an MVP that will take months to build, it's probably not minimum. If you can't explain your MVP in a couple of sentences, it's probably not minimum.

What you build also needs to be *viable*. You should think of viability in two ways: providing enough of an experience to show value to your customers, and providing enough information to you to prove or disprove a hypothesis. For example, some people think of buying Google AdWords as an MVP. I don't consider that a good MVP because all it tells you is that a person clicked on your link—it doesn't tell you why, and you can't assume that clicking indicates that he is willing to spend money.

As companies have written about their successful (and unsuccessful) experiments, some patterns in MVP types have emerged. Some common MVP types* include:

---

* Because these methods have emerged fairly organically, different people have come up with different names for them and different variations. I've seen Concierge MVPs called "manualization," Wizard of Oz MVPs called "Flinstone-ing," and Pre-Order MVPs called "smoke testing," to name a few. You can see some more subtle variations of MVPs at *http://scalemybusiness.com/the-ultimate-guide-to-minimum-viable-products/*.

- Pre-Order MVP

- Audience Building MVP

- Concierge MVP

- Wizard of Oz MVP

- Single Use Case MVP

- Other People's Product MVP

For each of these, we'll walk through what it is, provide an example of how it might work, and explain what you can learn from this style of experiment. We'll also describe situations where each type of MVP works well (hint: all of you can benefit from a Pre-Order MVP).

Pre-Order MVP

A Pre-Order MVP is where you describe the intended solution and solicit potential customers to sign up and order it before it is available. The Pre-Order MVP is not about gauging interest; it is about gauging commitment. Collecting email addresses or even survey data from prospective customers is not sufficient.

For any product or solution you wanted to build, you could create a website describing the problem you're solving. A Pre-Order MVP will often collect a credit card number with the promise that it will not be charged until the product is available.* In some enterprise situations, a letter of intent or agreement to roll out a pilot program may suffice as well.

Based on your costs and the investment required to pursue this product, you might decide that you will only proceed if more than a certain number of customers pre-order.

Kickstarter is a Pre-Order MVP. While it's primarily described as a crowd-funding platform, it is also effectively validating customer demand and willingness to commit financially to a solution. Even when the customer pledge amount is substantially less than the eventual product price, it is still a very strong signal. There is extremely high friction in getting customers to pay anything at all!

If thousands of people pledge money for a product that doesn't yet exist, that's a strong validation of demand. If the project can't raise its funding

---

* Some describe this as "vaporware" or "demoware," though I think of that term as having a slightly malicious intent. For example, a company might offer vague promises of future benefits that may never materialize in order to prevent customers from switching to a competitor.

goal, that suggests that the project is not solving a real problem for a sufficient number of customers.

Case Study: Finale Fireworks

As Marcus Gosling, now principal design architect at Salesforce.com, explains, "The best validation of a business hypothesis comes when someone takes her credit card out. In the formative months of Finale Fireworks, I traveled to Iowa along with the other two cofounders to attend the Pyrotechnic Guild International's annual fireworks convention."

Gosling and his cofounders had created a fireworks game and wanted to sell it. "We rented a tiny booth and showed a very basic demo of our fireworks game," said Gosling. "We quickly learned that fireworks people were not really interested in virtual fireworks. Instead, they wanted inexpensive software to design and trigger real shows. At that convention, we sold 60 prerelease copies of the software for 50% off. We hadn't even written the software yet. Those sales were the best possible validation that we had a product idea that people would pay for."

Use Cases

The Pre-Order MVP is the best way to validate that you're building something that customers will buy, hands down. Most products and companies should be looking for a way to implement a Pre-Order MVP, even if they've already used some of the MVP methods described earlier to validate their strategy. (The main exception I'll grant is for companies with high profiles that are dependent on first-mover advantage. It's hard for those companies to avoid press coverage, which creates distraction and often an advantage to competitors.)

Pre-Order MVPs work well for:

- Solutions that require a critical mass of customers in order to be sustainable or profitable

- Solutions that require a substantial outlay of time and resources to build

But really, almost all of you should be trying a Pre-Order MVP—whether it comes in the form of a pledge, a pre-order, a letter of intent, or a pilot program.

Audience Building MVP

The Audience Building MVP is a literal application of customer development: it involves building up a customer base in advance of building your product. Once you've identified a prospective customer base, you create a gathering place for them to come and get information, connect with like-minded people, and exchange ideas. As you observe your audience, you can measure what content, features, or people they engage most eagerly with. This allows you to validate demand for the features or services you'll eventually build. Once you're ready to release a product, you don't have to worry about publicity or distribution: you know exactly where to find your prospective customers.

Moz,* 37Signals, and Mint.com are all examples of companies that used blogging to build up communities in advance of releasing their products. All three companies, by the time they launched a scalable product, had a captive audience of thousands of relevant customers. It's unclear, however, whether these blogs were used as validation of the product concepts. (In other words, would Mint.com have decided to scrap its personal finance product if it was unable to attract enough readers to the MintLife blog?)

A clearer example of an Audience Building MVP as validation is seen in the recently launched Product Hunt website, which provides a leaderboard of the best new products every day. Founder Ryan Hoover invested just 20 minutes on an MVP to assess his potential audience. Hoover used Linkydink, a way to share links via email, to create a simple mailing list and invited a few dozen people. If he didn't see more mailing list signups, or if activity on the list petered out after a few days, Hoover was ready to conclude that the idea wasn't worth pursuing. Only once he saw a rise in signups, activity, and enthusiasm did he start building a rudimentary site. Product Hunt is a side project for Hoover, but in its first two months of life has already attracted over 4,000 users.†

Use Cases

The Audience Building MVP doesn't validate whether people are willing to spend money on your solution. However, you can measure customer retention and participation, which may be enough to justify an investment in developing a full solution. Audience building is also highly scalable: you are literally reaching out to your entire prospective customer base.

An Audience Building MVP works well for:

- Online products and services
- Free products or products that are inherently social

---

*   Moz recently rebranded; for the first 10 years it was known as SEOMoz.

†   *http://www.producthunt.co/*

- Teams with an abundance of content and community production skills
- Consulting businesses looking to extend into more scalable products or services
- Audiences who safeguard their time more than their money (e.g., doctors, venture capitalists, CEOs)

Concierge MVP

Named for the concierge who helps you out in a hotel, in a Concierge MVP, manual effort is used to solve the customer's problem. The customer knows that you are manually providing the solution. In exchange for a large investment of your personalized attention, she agrees to provide extensive feedback. The Concierge MVP allows you to offer the experience of using the product to customers before you actually build it.

Imagine that you saw an opportunity in connecting parents with customized, low-cost, educational activities for their kids. A Concierge MVP might entail contacting a half-dozen parents and having conversations with them about their children and how they choose activities for them. Armed with that information, you could manually research local activities and write up a list of recommendations for each parent.

This solution is not scalable at all: it would take hours per customer per week to provide your solution without automation. But what you learned during this intensive manual phase would dramatically reduce your risk.

You'd validate demand by following up personally to see which parents actually attended the suggested activities. You'd prioritize features by asking which pieces of information were critical (or missing) from your list. You might discover that your concierge clients consider this a "nice-to-have" service that they'd be unlikely to pay for. You would probably also discover that the criteria that parents use to choose activities for their children are not what you expected. All of this learning could occur before you started designing your site, writing code, or filling a database with information.

Case Study: StyleSeat

The stylists, spa owners, massage therapists, and other beauty professionals who make up StyleSeat's target market are busy people. Technology is not their expertise, their highest priority, or even their interest.

Dan Levine, CTO of StyleSeat explains, "For our customers, one of the most important factors in making a decision is 'Do I trust these people?' There is more than a little bit of fear around 'How do I make this work for me?'"

The initial hypothesis

StyleSeat started with the hypothesis that there had to be a better way for consumers to book stylist appointments and for these small business owners to promote themselves. But founders Melody McCloskey and Dan Levine knew they needed to learn more about the industry. They started by reaching out to a friend who owned a spa and asked her to invite all of her friends in the industry to come drink champagne and learn about technology from McCloskey and Levine.

That first meeting turned into weekly meetings where the founders taught their audience how to use Facebook, Twitter, and email to promote their businesses. "We almost became the 'Geek Squad' for these stylists, because that was the fastest way to learn their pain points," says Levine. "Going out there and immersing ourselves in the market is not only how we learned, but how we built trust among our customers."

Starting on the MVP

After the first few weeks, McCloskey and Levine learned enough about customer pain points to start building an MVP. For the next six months, they worked on customer development and product development in parallel. As they began building the product, they gradually shifted the focus of their customer conversations from validating hypotheses to validating the product with a group of beta users. "Watching people use our product was critical. We had to see how their minds worked when they used new tools."

Expanding the hypothesis

One of the biggest breakthroughs for StyleSeat was realizing that their opportunity was much larger than the original hypothesis. McCloskey and Levine had envisioned a tool that solved the scheduling pain point. But stylists "didn't want an app. Our customers didn't want Piece A here and Piece B there; they wanted everything in one place. It became abundantly clear; our customers needed a solution that helped their businesses grow. We changed our thinking from building 'a scheduling tool' to 'being *the* technology partner for the beauty industry.'"

McCloskey and Levine's deep understanding of customer needs helped drive the initial customer value experience. StyleSeat had identified that uploading photos and getting set up on Facebook was the perfect freemium hook. "From there, we asked a stylist if she want to reach her customers by email, and said that we offer these other services...it's easy to convince them to upgrade."

Ongoing customer development

After the initial six months of intensive customer development, StyleSeat continues to constantly work with customers to develop features and marketing. One tactic they use is to segment customers—most active users and new users—and reach out with a phone call. "We have a script, technically, but it's mostly just a conversation. What are people having trouble with? What do they like? If they're no longer using us, what were their initial expectations for the product?" These conversations fuel changes, which StyleSeat then validates using A/B testing.

Four years later, Levine is surprised by how closely the product mirrors that original MVP. What they learned in the first six months of working closely with customers allowed them to avoid mistakes and wrong turns. "It may have slowed down our initial development," says Levine, "but we've gained that time back and more."

Use Cases

Concierge MVPs are not scalable, but they allow you to validate demand for a product as well as challenge your assumptions on logistics and needed features.

Concierge MVPs work well for:

- Audiences that are offline or not technologically savvy

- Solutions where logistics are difficult to predict

- Solutions where it will be capital intensive to scale up operational investments

- Products or services where personalized customer satisfaction is a competitive differentiator

Wizard of Oz MVP

In a Wizard of Oz MVP, you provide a product that appears to be fully functional, but is actually powered by manual human effort. Unlike the Concierge MVP, the customer is not aware that a person is carrying out the tasks normally handled by software or automated processes.

Imagine that you want to solve the problem of allowing agile companies to localize their software more frequently. A Wizard of Oz MVP might present a few customers with an online dashboard where they could submit new text to be translated. But instead of an automated translation, you might have one or two Spanish speakers sitting in front of their computers waiting for a submission and quickly typing in translations on the fly.

Like the Concierge MVP, this solution is not scalable. But you could watch how customers interact with your fake dashboard, ask about the translation and turnaround speed and quality, and assess how much they would be willing to pay for your service.

Case Study: Porch.com

"We looked at the home improvement market and had certain ideas about what the right solution would be," says Matt Ehrlichman, CEO of Porch.com.

The team identified key assumptions about what homeowners wanted, customer acquisition, and built up data around pricing, and then set about creating an MVP. The company, originally called HelpScore.com, would help homeowners to find the best contractors and professionals for their home based on a scoring system.

The team built a Wizard of Oz MVP; its website appeared to be backed by a scoring algorithm. In reality, a team member was manually doing research and writing up a report. That information was presented in a web interface and the team watched how customers interacted with it and whether they converted.

Hypothesis invalidated

"We talked to homeowners, and our hypothesis was completely disproven. The score wasn't important at all. What people asked us was, 'Did my friends or neighbors use this contractor?' Homeowners wanted a sense of this professional's project history and the jobs they'd done in the past. They wanted word-of-mouth recommendations. It took us in a totally different direction."

Minimum exceptional product

The team changed the name to Porch. They continued to build MVPs for a couple of months until they felt confident that the product direction was validated. From there, they moved on to validating the content and channels they'd need to master to acquire customers profitably. "Lean is about reducing waste. You can waste the most time and energy if you're going down the wrong path. Now that we've validated our direction with data, we're confident and can invest more deeply down the right path. We shifted into stealth mode, amassing a tremendous amount of data that we knew customers wanted in order to make good decisions for finding home service professionals. We want to come back with something that does what it does well. We want to release a minimum *exceptional* product."

Porch launched in June 2013 and features data on more than 1.5 million home improvement professionals.

Use Cases

The Wizard of Oz MVP is an excellent method for validating customer behavior "in the wild." Because you're presenting what appears to be a complete solution, with no humans involved, you don't need to worry about customer behaviors being tainted by politeness. If your solution is useful, customers will try it; if not, they won't.

Wizard of Oz MVPs work well for:

- Solutions that will eventually require sophisticated algorithms or automation

- Potentially sensitive problem areas (finance, health, dating, legal)

- Two-sided markets where you can emulate one side to validate interest from the other*

Single Use Case MVP

A Single Use Case MVP is a working product or piece of technology that focuses on a *single* problem or task. This allows you to validate a single hypothesis.

Don't confuse "small" with "shoddy"—the Single Use Case MVP is *not* a license to build a bunch of features as quickly as possible by skipping over design and user experience. The point is to do one thing and do it well. (Remember, the "viable" part of MVP means you need to provide value to the customer!)

Imagine that you wanted to solve the problem of companies spending too much time on customer support. A Single Use Case MVP might entail selecting a single channel and type of problem to start with. For example, you might allow customers to create templated email responses to messages containing a set phrase like "cancel my account" or "update billing address."

This solution is scalable, but it's only a fraction of what you envision. It doesn't help with email that doesn't contain a set phrase, and it doesn't help with phone or live chat support. But it allows you to validate that customers are willing to use and even pay for the partial solution. As these early

---

* For example, I talked about LaunchBit in Chapter 6. LaunchBit is in a two-sided market because it needs to provide value to both the advertising networks and content publishers that it works with. Without the advertising networks, LaunchBit has no value to offer the content publishers; without publishers, it can't provide value to the ad networks.

customers demand more features, you can use their requests to help you prioritize which parts of the solution you build next.

With a Single Use Case MVP, your customers will complain, and that's a good thing. It means that customers have gotten some value from your product and they're ready for it to deliver more value.

If the customers using a Single Use Case MVP aren't complaining, it doesn't mean that they want more features. It means they aren't even seeing the potential for value. Throwing more features at them won't solve that problem. Instead, it's time to figure out why your highly focused hypothesis was wrong and how you can shift direction to get closer to what customers want.

Case Study: Hotwire

Hotwire was facing a challenge: its hotel bookings site was showing its age after 10 years of new features and workflows.

Product manager Kristen Mirenda and interaction designer Karl Schultz were able to form a clear hypothesis after observing customers interacting with Hotwire.com.

"Customers trying to use Hotwire to book a hotel abandon the process because they cannot figure out where their prospective hotel will be located. Map-centric search results should help increase hotel booking conversions."

But that would require a massive change to the interaction of the current Hotwire.com site. No one was comfortable making a change of that magnitude overnight. "Hotwire's hotel bookings bring in a large portion of the company's revenue," explains Mirenda.

Map-based search results on a shadow site

Instead, Mirenda, Schultz, and lead engineer Jim Tay led an effort to create a "shadow site" that would allow them to test their hypotheses on a very small percentage of Hotwire's existing traffic.

They built an MVP version of the site centered around map-based search results. "The first version had no design, and you couldn't sort or filter or even revise your search. None of those things mattered for our hypothesis around map usage."

The site was designed so that a variable percentage of Hotwire's normal traffic could be redirected to the new design. People who landed on the new site did not realize that they were part of an experimental group, though the new design did include a link to offer feedback (see Figure 7-1).

The first version of their MVP launched to just 1% of the customers coming to Hotwire.com. "It definitely put us outside our comfort zone to put something like that out into the world. We built in the ability to shut it off within hours, just in case," says Miranda.

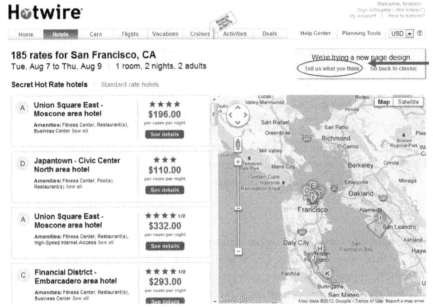

Figure 7-1. Version 1 of Hotwire's MVP lacked features, but validated the hypothesis that map-based search results provided a better customer experience and could ultimately be more profitable

Iterating on the MVP

Customer feedback on the experimental Hotwire site was mostly negative, focused on the missing sort and filter functionality, not on the big map in the center of the screen. And people were still booking hotels! Map engagement was up, and conversion for the experimental group only went down 17%—not bad for a completely unoptimized, feature-poor MVP.

Revising the MVP to solve pain points

As soon as the team had enough data to guide the next iteration, they turned off the 1% experiment and started building to solve for the next biggest pain points: lack of sorting and filtering. With each successive release, performance improved and the team was able to increase the size of the experimental group and get faster results.

Nonetheless, Mirenda and Schultz struggled a bit for acceptance within the company. Mirenda says, "As the first team to go lean, we hit all the potholes! For each mistake, we had measured validation for what not to do the next time—but that's not what people were accustomed to. People weren't used to hearing customer complaints—even if they didn't affect overall usage." Schultz agrees, "The benefits [of working lean] have to be shared widely so people can understand the value."

The new site gains traction

Gradually the percentage of people who saw the new Hotwire site was at 50%, and performance caught up to the original site.

Hotwire has now adopted the new site with map-based search results for both the United States and international audiences. As the team continued to optimize, conversion rates continued to increase. Hotwire is a subsidiary of Expedia, which earned $4 billion in revenues in 2012.

Use Cases

The Single Use Case MVP forces you to focus on a single solution area. Not only is this faster to build, but it's also simpler to explain to prospective customers. There is far lower perceived friction in trying a new product or solution that does just one thing.

Single Use Case MVPs work well for:

- Existing products and companies that need to validate a change in direction or a spinoff product

- Trying to enter a market dominated by a larger, more complicated, more expensive product

- Validating how your product can create the most value for your customers

Other People's Product MVP

The Other People's Product MVP is where you use parts of an existing product or service to validate your ideas. In some cases, this is a variation of the Wizard of Oz MVP, where you may offer your customers a solution and then manually use a competitor's tools or infrastructure to fulfill it. In other cases, it may involve using an existing API or framework to more quickly build a solution.

The defining feature of the Other People's Product MVP is that you are piggybacking on competitors who are already solving the problem, as a way to more quickly learn and validate ideas.

For example, if you wanted to solve some of the problems with the taxi industry, you might sign up to be an UberX driver. In doing so, you're not only spending your time but even making money for your competition! However, you would quickly learn which aspects of the service mattered and could talk to customers in order to identify opportunities for differentiation. By relying on an existing product's marketing and infrastructure, you could hugely reduce the cost of learning.

Case Study: Bing Offers

"Imagine it's 4 p.m. and business is slow; the merchant can pull out her phone, create a deal, and, as you're walking past the business, you see it."

That's one of the opportunities that engineer Guy Shahine and others envisioned for Bing in the local advertising space.

The team had a vision for a platform offering real-time deals. But the Bing Offers team quickly ran into roadblocks when they started developing an offers app. "Merchants didn't want to use it until users were there," says Shahine, "but users wouldn't install an app to get deals unless merchants were participating."

Roadblocks lead to pivot

That realization led to the team's first pivot. Rather than investing effort in soliciting merchants for deals, they piggybacked on deals from competitors like LivingSocial, Yelp, and Amazon Local. "The pitch was easy; we just told them, 'We'll put your deals in front of more eyes,'" explains Shahine. This allowed the Bing Offers team to start testing the service with real customers in a matter of weeks, not months.

An opportunity to make deals easy for customers

"People got confused when we sent them to other deal sites. They complained about problems they'd previously experienced with other services like Groupon—buying a deal and then forgetting about it and having it expire or being on a date and being embarrassed to have to tell the waiter you have a discount. They didn't want to have to check the site every day to look for deals. We realized that we could provide a superior experience by just linking deals to a customer's credit card; they swipe the card, and they get the deal automatically with no friction."

For Shahine and others who'd worked at Microsoft for years, using a lean approach was refreshing. "We had a strong product vision, but not a detailed six-month plan. We did everything in two-week sprints, and we didn't plan more than two sprints in advance." This allowed the team to iterate based on feedback from the customers testing the app. For example, people hesitated when the app prompted them to enter their credit card number to enable the automatic discounts: "People thought we were going to charge them for something and stopped the setup process." This led to a quick change to the home page to clarify that credit card numbers were only for processing discounts, not for charges.

Keep learning from customers

As the team builds out the app and service, they continue to learn from customers in a variety of ways—including analytics tools like Omniture and Crazy Egg, feedback tools like UserVoice, and hands-on observation.

"Today I can go on the weekend to a coffee shop and let people play around with Bing Offers and come into the office on Monday with feedback, and we can roll in tweaks within a few days," says Shahine. "It's a big change from Waterfall: a bunch of design architects spending a year on design reviews and then saying 'go build this.' It's definitely a cultural shift, but so far, I'm seeing a lot more buy-in [for the lean methodology here at Microsoft]. You learn a lot as you apply it, and it makes your job more fun."

Use Cases

The Other People's Product MVP allows you to learn and validate quickly using competitor resources as building blocks. Not only does this reduce the time and resources you need to invest, but it also forces you to learn more about your competition and identify potential advantages that you can wield against them.

Other People's Product MVPs work well for:

- Entering a space with established competitors
- Solutions where logistics are difficult to predict
- Teams with limited engineering resources

We've Built an MVP, Now What?

In the beginning of this chapter, I talked about the importance of identifying your highest risk factors. Hopefully you built an MVP that helped you to answer some of your most pressing questions around distribution, value, business model, and functionality.

Most likely, at least some of your assumptions were shattered when your customers actually interacted with your MVP. Perhaps customers loved the functionality but balked at your price point; perhaps they were unconvinced by the prospective value proposition. The good news is that you almost certainly know more about your market and product than you did before.

Armed with your new knowledge, look at your hypotheses again. Which ones have you validated? Which ones were incorrect? For each incorrect hypothesis, what information have you gained about why it was incorrect? Based on this updated information, you can now formulate a more educated set of hypotheses.

In some cases, you may want to conduct customer interviews with a different audience. In others, it may be more appropriate to devise a different MVP that helps you learn about other aspects of your business.

There is unfortunately no magic dividing line between "yes, you've validated your MVP and your product will be successful" and "no, back to the drawing board." It's all one big gray area where you gradually gain more and more evidence that you're on the right track.

For this reason, there is no point where you should stop doing customer development entirely. Even once you've made big "irreversible" decisions (we're definitely building this service, we just hired an engineer, we quit our day jobs), you will benefit from continuously learning and validating.

In the next chapter, we'll talk about ways to use customer development after you've already built a product, collected revenues, and developed relationships with your customers.

Key Takeaways

- When building an MVP, think about how the customer will measure the value she gets from the product.

- Stick to minimum: don't include full functionality.

- Pre-order MVPs involve customers paying for the MVP in some way; try this in one form or another, whether the payment is a pledge, a pre-order, a letter of intent, or a pilot program.

- Audience Building MVPs help build a market.

- Concierge MVPs and Wizard of Oz MVPs solve problems manually to validate that there's a market.

- Single Use Case MVPs solve part of a customer's problem or focus on a single feature.

- Other People's Product MVPs let you piggyback on others' ideas while validating demand among your customers.

CHAPTER 8

How Does Customer Development Work When You Already Have Customers?

In the medical industry, things revolve around sales cycles that extend into the 18-month zone. Doctors are unforgiving, unable to articulate what they want, and if you iterate with them, they are unforgiving.

—Henry Wei, Senior Medical Director of Clinical Innovation at Aetna

The ability to learn faster than your competitors may be the only sustainable competitive advantage.

—Arie de Geus, former head of Shell Oil's Strategic Planning Group

If you work at a large company with existing customers, I know what you're thinking. *There's no way these techniques would work for me*: I can't go into customer meetings with guesses. If I talk about new ideas, they will assume the ideas are product directions. They'll either want to buy the product tomorrow or get upset if they don't like the new direction. I can't take up an important customer's time and ask a bunch of questions without having anything to show him.

It's true: you probably can't practice customer development in exactly the same way that an early-stage startup can. You'll need to adapt the process a bit, just as GE, Microsoft, Aetna, Intuit, and the US government have.

For those readers who are working with a brand-new customer base or within a small startup, you may wish to skim this chapter and return later in your company's lifecycle. The techniques described in this chapter are fairly conservative, and as such, will not allow you to learn and reduce risk as quickly as the interview and analysis tactics in Chapters 1 through 7 and the Appendix will.

In this chapter, we'll talk about adapting customer development tactics to work effectively even with customers who bring inflexibility, constraints, and pre-existing expectations along with their dollars. We'll also talk about how to set appropriate expectations and reduce bias. We'll describe targeted tactics, including:

- How to adapt the concept of minimum viable product (MVP)

- Finding the right customers to talk to

- Nondisruptive ways to introduce new products

- Techniques for learning how customers really use your product

By the end of this chapter, you'll have a clearer sense of how to practice customer development to minimize risk and maximize learning for your organization.

Adapting the MVP Concept

What works for small startups may not work for you.

When you read blog posts about startups using lean tactics, you'll hear about methods like this one used by TripAdvisor CMO Barbara Messing. When Messing wants to assess interest in a specific type of travel package, she posts banner ads advertising it on TripAdvisor's site. If people don't click on it, it's not worth pursuing. If they do click on it, they get a 404 (Not Found) error. If enough of them click on the banner, TripAdvisor creates the offering.* It's an effective and low-cost way to assess customer demand, but if you wouldn't feel comfortable doing the same on your site, you're not alone.

---

* *http://blogs.hbr.org/cs/2013/03/four_ways_to_market_like_a_sta.html*

Nothing Broken

If you add nonfunctional experiences to an existing product or website, you also make it harder to use and less rewarding. For customers who are evaluating your product based on reliability and credibility, a broken link or dead end makes them wonder, "What else can't I trust in this product?"

For example, years ago I was moderating usability test sessions for a financial services application that I had just redesigned. User response was unexpectedly dismal and I had no idea why. One participant immediately told me, "I would never use this website."

Why not?

He pointed to the bottom of the screen. "There's no privacy link," he said.

Was I talking to a privacy nutcase? I wondered to myself, and asked, "How important is it to you to read the privacy policy before using a website?"

He looked baffled, and said, "All I know is, bank websites are supposed to have that little picture of a lock and a privacy link at the bottom, or else you're not supposed to use them."

By accidentally omitting one tiny credibility marker, I had inadvertently tainted customer reactions to the product. Before the next participant arrived, I quickly added in a lock image and a fake privacy policy link to the demo. Customer feedback immediately flipped from strongly negative to positive.

Even if you're working on a standalone demo, you may be dealing with customers who have exacting standards. I've seen executives who get riled up over a typo on a PowerPoint slide. In the startup world, the phrase "If you're not embarrassed by your first version, you waited too long to release" gets thrown around a lot. In the enterprise world, if you are embarrassed by your first version, you may not get the chance to show a second version. Invest a few extra hours in spellchecking, making sure your links aren't broken, and cleaning up your images.

Attractive but Fake

On the other hand, if you make a demo or prototype look *too* good, you run the risk of customers thinking it's already built (or in the process of being built). They may delay purchases or upgrades assuming they can just wait for the new version. Then what happens if you invalidate your hypothesis and decide not to build the product or feature after all? You may wind up with customers who are disappointed and angry.

Use a sketch

Even if you've clearly explained that you are doing research to find out what customers want and not showing a product direction, and reiterated that what they will see is subject to change, it's psychologically hard to see something and then lose it. A useful way around this is to create something that looks good, but is clearly fake. You may want to use a program like Balsamiq, which allows you to quickly create consistent, clear, but cartoon-like sketches. No one seeing a Balsamiq mockup (Figure 8-1) mistakes it for a finished product.

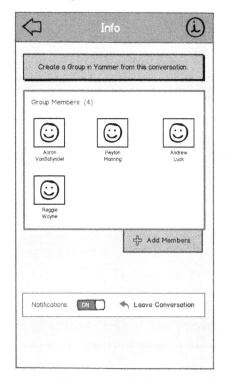

Figure 8-1. Balsamiq wireframes approximate layout and interactions but are clearly not working versions

Use a different domain

If you need to show more high-fidelity images, one approach is to use a different domain name and branding. Your fake domain can look elegant and well-designed as long as it doesn't look like your company's design. At both Yodlee and KISSmetrics, we used alternate domains to test prototypes before committing to build the real products.

More Viable than Minimum

Companies with existing customers need to define MVP a bit differently than a startup would.

At Aetna, product development uses the term "minimum sellable product." At Yammer, we emphasize the word *viable*. It's OK—even required—to go a little bit above and beyond the minimum to create a cohesive experience.

It's different for startups

For startups, an MVP is the minimum amount of product that provokes a nonneutral response. That's because new companies face different risks than established companies. As Steve Blank says, "On Day One, a start-up has no customers.... On Day One, a startup is a *faith-based initiative* built on guesses."* For a startup, the first risk to overcome is "Will anyone care enough to respond to this idea?" Even a tiny confirmation of interest like clicking a link or scrolling down a page is something a startup can't count on.

In the TripAdvisor example, that could be a banner ad that people either click or do not click. Not clicking is a neutral response: it shows that people aren't even curious enough to notice the potential product. On the other hand, clicking doesn't really tell you all that much. It tells you that people are curious, somewhat interested, or that they noticed the ad. It doesn't tell you that they are likely to whip out a credit card and book some travel (Figure 8-2).

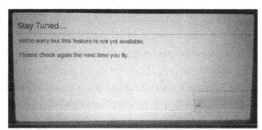

Figure 8-2. The result when I clicked the "read" button on a Virgin America in-flight entertainment console; unfortunately, there's no way for Virgin to know whether customers secretly long for books or are just bored and pressing buttons

* *http://steveblank.com/2012/05/14/9-deadliest-start-up-sins/*

You know someone cares

If you've already got a product and customers, you've already mitigated the "Does anyone care at all?" risk. You can safely assume that your customers will care at least a little bit. You need to learn more from your MVP.

At Yammer, now a part of Microsoft, we define an MVP as "the smallest amount of product we need to build to provide value and learn something about how a person behaves in this context." A *minimum viable feature* allows a customer to complete an interaction. We can use analytics to measure whether they returned and repeated that interaction, or we can use qualitative user research to learn how they felt about it. The most successful approach is often a combination of both.

For Yammer, a successful MVP is one that allows us to conclude "this is probably an idea worth investing more effort in, and here's why" (or "this is probably not worth pursuing, and here's why").

A little beyond minimum: user complaints, but not frustration

If the customer feels disappointed or frustrated, it's not a sufficient MVP. On the other hand, if a customer complains, that's a good thing.

> *Complaining is a sign of interest. It shows that the customer values the experience enough that she wants it to improve so that she can continue using it.*

Watch out for those who can't stop at minimum

If the product managers or designers start adding *"but what if...?"* use cases, that is definitely going beyond minimum. In general, product managers and designers who are not accustomed to lean startup principles have a hard time stopping at minimum. They're used to designing fully thought-out working products. Minimum versions won't feel comfortable to them. Actually, minimum versions don't feel comfortable to anyone.

Here's a case where we distinguished carefully between minimum and comprehensive features. When Yammer introduced a lightweight collaborative editing feature, we wanted answers to two questions before creating a full feature: Would people use the functionality? Would the experience of collaborative editing feel comfortable and provide value?

To answer those questions, we needed to provide a complete, uninterrupted workflow for a few key tasks:

- Creating a document
- Editing the document
- Inviting others to coedit the document

- Distinguishing one person's edits from another person's
- Saving changes

Many additional tasks were excluded from the first version. There was no delete capability, no version history, and no method for sharing or emailing the document.

That was an uncomfortable release! No one liked the idea of being able to create a note and then being unable to delete it. However, we recognized that our biggest risk was that no one would use the feature at all. If no one used the feature to edit documents, no one would ever have documents to delete or share. The lack of a delete feature was annoying, but something that users would only discover after having used the feature.

Those capabilities were needed for a mature feature, but not to validate the initial value proposition. Only once the initial need was validated did we invest further development effort in building out those secondary use cases.

Common Objections to MVPs

As the practice of building MVPs has become more accepted across teams within Microsoft, I have encountered a number of common objections:

Objection: Our customers have higher expectations of us, so we can't deliver an MVP.

Response: MVP doesn't mean that we're delivering a broken experience. The design and functionality can be high quality; we are just supporting fewer use cases. If our hypothesis is correct, we are delivering some value to our customers now, and we'll add more value later. If our hypothesis is not correct, we are delivering a small feature that isn't valuable instead of a large feature that still isn't valuable.

I have actually stopped using the term "minimum viable product" entirely when talking with internal Microsoft teams. It simply took too long to explain that MVP was not a synonym for subpar. Instead, I frame what we do as "hypothesis-driven development," which puts the emphasis on validation of ideas as opposed to product quality.*

---

* Cindy Alvarez and Ethan Gur-esh, Principal Program Manager, talk at the 2013 Lean Startup Conference on how Microsoft is adopting lean principles, *http://www.youtube.com/watch?v=nD-JLrza1KU*.

Objection: We have to support all platforms.

Response: If we built a feature only for Android, and no one used it, should we feel bad that we didn't also build that same useless feature for iOS and Windows Phone and MacOS and Windows 8? Assuming the feature tests well, we can quickly add it to all other platforms.

Objection: We have to scale to millions of users.

Response: We are validating the product on a subset of our customer base. If only thousands of customers have access to the product, it only needs to be high-performance enough to support thousands of customers. It's a waste of engineering resources to overengineer a product that customers may never buy. Assuming we validate customer demand, we can increase performance before opening access to our entire customer base.

Objection: There is no smaller subset of features that will satisfy our customers.

Response: This isn't the only release we're ever going to do. Let's think in terms of how we can provide the most value with the smallest investment of time. Are some features used by a greater percentage of customers than others? Are some features used daily while others are used weekly or less frequently? By starting with the absolute highest-priority features, we can start learning and validating our ideas quickly. As customers request the missing features, we can use those requests to help us prioritize the order in which we build them.

Objection: We can't introduce inconsistency into the design.

Response: Maintaining design consistency is incredibly high risk. It means either stagnating for long periods of time, or investing in high-cost full redesigns that may actually hurt usage and usability. It's also hard for us to get design changes prioritized over new features. If we can show that a small design change measurably helps customers use our product, we can more easily argue for additional design improvements across the rest of the product.

> In my experience, these responses help keep the conversation go-
> ing. They don't guarantee that your product team will successfully
> overcome all objections and be able to build MVPs.
>
> In a big company, it's incredibly hard to overcome all of the factors
> that can stand in the way of practicing customer development.
> Still, every small success offers evidence to the next project team
> that this method of development works to reduce risk and build
> better products.

Finding the Right Customers

Chapter 3 talked about earlyvangelists, those customers with such a strong
pain point that they are eager to give feedback and try even the earliest,
most bare-bones version of your solution. Earlyvangelists are critical to
helping startups get their product off the ground initially, but they may or
may not end up being their most valuable customers later on. It's critical,
once you have a product and customers, to reassess who your most valuable
and passionate customers are.

So who are your best customers? You may have thought of your earliest
adopters, the ones who wrote you the biggest checks, the ones who never
complain, or the ones with the most influence or most recognizable brand
names. That's not the right way to figure out who your *best* customers are
(this is true for any company, even those not doing customer development).*

How I Learned to Find the Right Customers by Finding the Wrong Ones

I'll explain how important it is to choose the right customers by telling you
just what happened to me when I chose the *wrong* sort of customers.

At Yodlee, I made the mistake of giving demos of new prospective product
ideas to a few of our more conservative customers. I'll let you in on exactly
what we were thinking because it's a really common misconception:

> *They are big-name customers. If we meet their needs and incorpo-*
> *rate their feedback, they could be powerful reference customers and*
> *likely bring in others. They've been slow to upgrade, but maybe that's*

---

* I go into more detail on why the seemingly best customers aren't and what a mutually
beneficial customer looks like here: *http://www.cindyalvarez.com/decisionmaking/your-best-
customers-probably-arent.*

because we haven't given them anything to get excited about. We'll show them how our thinking has evolved and get them re-energized!

Those demos did not go well: the customers were so unreceptive to new ideas that they could not provide any useful answers. The implications for the relationship were even worse. These customers were afraid that we were going to turn our backs on the product they were using and getting value from. They were anxious that they were going to be stuck with a dead-end product while we directed all our innovation energy elsewhere. We spent a lot of time doing damage control afterward.

What worked better for me back then was to collaborate with our account managers. Which customers are comfortable with change? Which ones engage us frequently (even if they're often complaining)? Which ones ask questions about our future product direction? I would then reach out to these customers, explaining that we were exploring a new direction and wanted to learn more from them.

Subscription billing provider Recurly taps into its customer support team's insights in a similar way: "[Support] knows which customers are beta-tolerant and interested in specific features, so we can show them early prototypes and watch how they're using the product today."

Find the People Who Can't Live Without Your Product

Choosing customers based on our existing relationships was a more appropriate approach than choosing them based on account size or brand name. But the quality of an existing relationship isn't the best metric to use. It's also not applicable for many products and services—mass-produced physical goods, low-touch services, consumer software, and plenty of other businesses simply don't have a regular communication channel with customers.

Your best customers are the people who are getting the most value from your product. Sean Ellis, CEO of Qualaroo, developed a simple set of survey questions to identify the most passionate users of his products. You can create your own version of the eight-question survey for free at *http://www. survey.io*, but the most critical question is this one: How would you feel if you could no longer use our product? (See Figure 8-3.)*

---

* In my experience, asking "How disappointed would you be if you could no longer use [product]?" has been markedly more effective than asking the same question framed positively (How satisfied are you?/How would you rate?). I suspect the reason is a phenomenon called loss aversion: "Loss aversion is the simple idea that the misery produced by losing something that we feel is ours—say, money—outweighs the happiness of gaining the same amount of money." See Dan Ariely, *The Upside of Irrationality: The Unexpected Benefits of Defying Logic at Work and at Home*, p. 32.

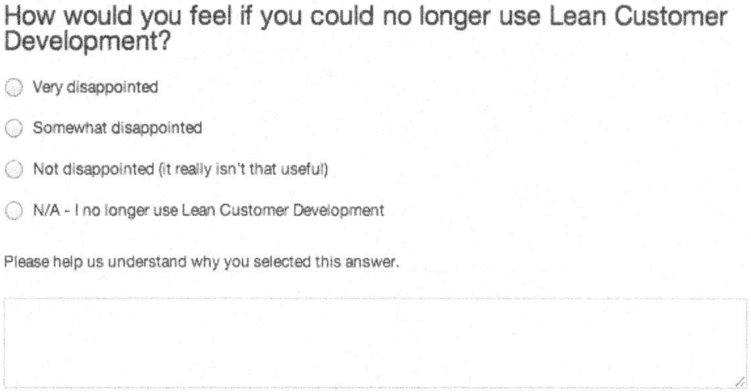

How would you feel if you could no longer use Lean Customer Development?

○ Very disappointed

○ Somewhat disappointed

○ Not disappointed (it really isn't that useful!)

○ N/A - I no longer use Lean Customer Development

Please help us understand why you selected this answer.

Figure 8-3. The "how disappointed" question from Sean Ellis' Customer Development Survey at http://survey.io

Find out who would answer "very disappointed." Those are the customers you should reach out to and learn from.

Those are the people who are the most passionate, who consider you almost more of a partner than a vendor. (That doesn't just apply to enterprise products; think of any friend who eagerly recommends his neighborhood butcher, his favorite energy drink, that amazing music-finding service.)

At Yammer, we use data to identify our most passionate users. Our analytics team segments the top 1% and top 10% of people who return and actively participate, and our user research team samples those populations to collect net promoter scores* as well as to engage in customer interviews to learn more about how they use Yammer, what their work environments are like, and how we could make their lives better.

Your Best Customers Hate Disruption

You're trying to take an existing product in a new direction.

You're trying to launch a new product that works differently but offers tremendously better value than an existing one.

---

* Net promoter score is a customer loyalty metric based on the question "How likely would you be to recommend our company/product/service to your friends and colleagues?" The score is based on a 0–10 scale and calculated by subtracting the total of your detractors (people who rate you a 6 or below) from your promoters (people who rate you a 9 or 10).

Your first instinct is probably to seek out your best customers—the ones who have loyally used your products for years. After all, who better understands the problem space?

Yes and no. Longtime customers are terrific at answering objective questions, providing reference information, and facilitating warm introductions to other prospective customers. However, their experiences and needs are often drastically different from those of your new or mainstream customers.

Why? Because they have invested significant effort in learning the product you already have. Even if it's deficient in some ways, they have developed workarounds and built their processes around the product that exists today. For that reason, loyal customers are extremely resistant to disruption.

John Gourville, a marketing professor at Harvard Business School, writes, "Rather than target professional photographers and serious amateurs with his first Kodak camera, in 1888, [Eastman] marketed his innovations to first-time buyers. In doing so, he was encouraging behavior among nonusers rather than trying to change entrenched behavior among existing users.... In fact, professional photographers and serious amateurs came to resent Eastman's cameras, largely because they offered a set of benefits they had learned to live without (e.g., ease of use, convenience) and sacrificed a set of benefits that had become part of their status quo (e.g., exclusivity, prestige)."

Here we have evidence of terrific customer development techniques dating back nearly 150 years!

Of course, it's no accident that I chose a quote about Kodak. Despite those auspicious beginnings, Kodak ensured its own self-destruction over the past few decades. Kodak engineer Steve Sasson invented the first digital camera back in 1975, but the company failed to pursue the technology and disrupt its profitable film camera business.* Kodak declared bankruptcy in 2012.

---

* Kodak could've used an organization-wide dedication to customer development: "Besides never capitalizing on the digital-camera tech it helped create, Kodak also gravely misunderstood the new ways consumers wanted to interact with their photos, the technologies involved, and the market forces surrounding them" (http://mashable.com/2012/01/20/kodak-digital-missteps/).

Customers Say the Magic Words

It's always been my experience that the words that your most enthusiastic customers use will be the words that other customers respond to immediately. The words that customers use are not the same words that a marketing team would use. Customers don't talk about features—they talk about the benefits they're getting, the feeling they get from using your product, what it replaces, and how much better their life is. When you echo *those* words back to other prospective customers, they get it.

Sal Virani, creator of Leancamp, asks customers three great questions:

- How likely would you be to recommend us?

- Who would you recommend us to?

- Imagine you're speaking to them. How would you describe us to them?

The second question is key—if the customer's vision of your target customer differs from yours, you should find out why! The emphasis on "speaking" is also important—it gives people permission to be natural and informal.

Virani writes, "I test their phrases in my advertising, headlines, and copy. It almost always gets a significant conversion uplift."*

Real Customer Intelligence

Words that customers choose to describe the product can help you sell more of it.

Features that customers mention (or fail to mention) can help you prioritize where to focus your future product development.

You don't need a formal survey; at the end of any customer interaction, you can ask the customers, "How would you describe this product?" I've asked it at the end of sales demos, customer support emails, and usability testing sessions. You can ask it when you run into customers at conferences or spot one using your product in the wild. I've even asked people who interview for jobs at my company! (See Chapter 9 for more ideas on how to work a little customer development into your interactions with customers.)

---

* *http://www.saintsal.com/2012/10/a-simple-way-to-truly-understand-why-your-customers-buy/*

How Customers Lower Your Market Risk

What's the biggest risk to most products? It's not that your product isn't good enough: it's that customers aren't even interested enough to try it.

Customers can't get value from your product until they use it. And given that you're competing with a million other things, it's incredibly hard to grab their attention. Your product might legitimately be the best, but what does that matter when every other product is making the same claim?

Customer development enables you to understand your target market's pain points and come up with solutions. But that's not the same as capturing the way your product makes customers *feel*.

Kathy Sierra talks about the important distinction between selling a great product and selling a product that makes great users. As people who build products, we're naturally biased to want to talk about features, technical sophistication, and triumphs of design and engineering. What our customers want is to hear that they'll feel smarter, get their jobs done faster, look better, feel less stressed, or get to replace an unwanted solution. When you echo those words back to other prospective customers, they get it (Figure 8-4).

The best person to sell to your customer is…your customer.

Figure 8-4. Your focus should be on making your customers feel awesome, not on telling customers that your products are awesome; http://headrush.typepad.com/

Once You've Found Your Customers, Explain, Explain, Explain

You'll need your customers to feel comfortable and excited about the customer development process. That's easy as long as you set expectations appropriately, which requires that you overcommunicate what you're doing, how customers participate, and how you'll use the information you get.

Whether you realize it or not, your initial hypothesis is uninformed by reality. You know your industry and you know your customers, but that doesn't prevent you from building products that don't meet customer needs. If it did, we'd never have seen New Coke, Qwikster, or the Segway.*

You're Asking Questions—Not Building Something

Customers are not accustomed to products changing direction. They're accustomed to hearing vendors sell, not ask. This is doubly true in the enterprise software space. Unless you are extremely clear in your communications, customers will interpret your questions as a commitment to build something. They see demos as a window into what is coming, not an exploration of what is possible.

To understand the impact of the need to overcommunicate, consider what would happen if you were at your favorite pizza place and the manager came over to ask you about burgers. Lacking context, you'd probably give inaccurate answers. Perhaps you'd say no or rush through answers because right now, all you can think about is pepperoni and four-cheese. Or you'd answer based on your weekend situation (buying lunch for your kid's soccer team full of picky eaters) as opposed to your weekday situation (working lunches with beer and premium burgers). Or you'd come back to the restaurant expecting to see burgers on the menu and be annoyed if they're not served. Or you'd avoid the restaurant, assuming that the pizza quality will decline once the kitchen is split between pizza and burgers. The restaurant would need to explain why they're asking, emphasize that they're learning from customers, and clarify that no changes are being made yet.

Even if your hypothesis is not out-and-out wrong, it's going to be significantly modified based on the real-world feedback you get during this process. The features you think are most important are probably *not* the most

---

* See *http://www.time.com/time/business/article/0,8599,186660-1,00.html*. There were numerous reasons why the Segway failed to take off, including a high price point and ambiguity over where you could ride it and whether you needed a license. Possibly the most convincing reason is the one that venture capitalist and essayist Paul Graham points out: "People don't want to be seen riding them. Someone riding a Segway looks like a dork" (*http://www.paulgraham.com/segway.html*).

important to the customer. One customer will rave about a feature that others consider trivial. Your emphasis will inevitably change, and you definitely don't want to make promises you can't keep.

You also don't want customers to feel that they should be polite. In many business and cultural settings, complaining is viewed as rude or unprofessional. As one Yammer user told me, "When I give feedback in surveys, I try to only say as many negative things as I can say a nice thing to balance it out." (Yikes. Presumably the worse your product is, the less honesty you'll get from her.)

What does that mean for your conversation with customers? It means you need to clearly communicate three things:

- Make it clear that you're here to learn
- Firmly state that all conversations are exploratory
- Give the customer permission to complain

It's important to state these points clearly and firmly from the beginning, and reiterate them throughout your conversations.

Here's a template that I've used recently for Yammer customers:

> On the Yammer product team, we are *exploring* some *new ideas* in the area of _____. In order to ensure that we have a deep *understanding* of our customers' needs, I would like to schedule some time with you to ask a few questions and get feedback on some *initial ideas*. We are *quite a ways from making any new product decisions*, but would benefit from your expertise.
>
> What I'd like to do is ask a few questions—no more than 20 minutes— and then walk you through a few *very rough prototype* slides. Are you available for a 45-minute call/meeting?

I've emphasized some of the words here (not in my email) because I want you to see how I'm weaving in the expectation that this is exploratory by using words that imply a distant future. This serves as a second qualification; it weeds out customers who are motivated by asking for specific roadmap enhancements. It's not useful to talk with customers who have an agenda to push for a specific feature.

Once a customer agrees to have an exploratory conversation, I start by mentioning that we extended this invitation only to a limited number of our most visionary customers. This sense of scarcity seems to encourage more specific, deep feedback. It also motivates people to refrain from sharing information with other customers or on social media. (Your lawyers will probably want you to get an NDA signed before you show anything to customers regardless.)

Say It Again: This Is Exploratory

During your conversations, you'll probably hear customers ask, "So when is this going to be available?" or "How likely are you to build this?" Don't give a politely noncommittal response with room for misinterpretation. It feels a bit awkward at first, but you must clearly repeat that this is exploratory.

Henry Wei, Senior Medical Director of Clinical Innovation at Aetna, agrees. "We have to be very explicit and say 'We're trying to figure out what you really need. We're not trying to rush this into existence if it's not what our customers will get value from.'"

It may take some practice, but ultimately you'll find that many of your customers will appreciate this style of discourse. Customers are often promised features and fixes. While they may hear promises from their vendors, those promises tend to fade after the sale closes. It's rare that customers hear from a vendor who is actively trying to identify and address their problems.

Being invited to talk about their specific experiences drives a level of customer involvement and engagement that nothing else can touch.

Such listening also yields another gift you can give to your customers: the ability to know just a little bit about what their competitors are thinking. We commonly anonymize what we've learned and then share a summary with customers we talked to. (For example, "We talked to 22 customers, including 15 Fortune 500 companies, and the major concerns we heard were X and Y.")

The Storytelling Demo

Here's the paradox with existing customers: it's hard to get their attention, or their feedback, unless you show them something visual. But as soon as a customer sees something, they think it's real. There's nothing new about showing slide decks to customers long before you start building the product. The problem is, as soon as customers see something, it becomes real in their minds. They leap to asking about specific features and functionality. You find yourself defending product decisions that you haven't even made yet—and you lose the opportunity to learn about the customer's problems and needs.

There's a solution to this problem: storytelling.

To stay in control of the conversation, you need to tell a story. Tell the story of one specific user and how she would use this product.

I've used the storytelling demo at Yodlee, at KISSmetrics, and at Yammer. User experience professionals will recognize this as a persona walkthrough.* However, personas are typically used internally to illustrate the needs of a representative user. In this scenario, you'll be talking to that representative user and inviting her to question or disagree with your demo.

By taking the perspective of a single representative user, you discourage the customer from thinking in terms of features or edge cases. Instead, you're guiding her to think through the workflow and tell you whether it makes sense.

Recently I've used the storytelling demo to show how Jessica, an archetypal user, would use Yammer.

I literally start the conversation with, "This is Jessica. She's a fictional employee of yours. I'm going to walk through how Jessica would use the new functionality we're working on." On each screen, I explain how Jessica works, what she's thinking, and how she's going to use specific features. To get a clearer sense of how this would flow, my sample script is included in the Appendix (see "Using a Storytelling Demo").

—— NOTE ——————————————————————

What you need:

- Identify the key features or concepts you need to validate.
- Write a script connecting the features in a way that makes sense, including names for the elements that Jessica interacts with, such as people, filenames, descriptors, and so on. Use a realistic task, such as "paying the bills" or "collaborating with coworkers on a presentation."
- Build a cohesive prototype that demonstrates all of these features or concepts. Your prototype needs to be consistent: if Jessica is editing a file called Sales Prospects on screen 2, it can't be called Meeting Notes on screen 3.
- Your demo should include all of the steps that Jessica needs to take. It doesn't need to be working code, but it needs to feel clickable and not skip steps.
- We use Invision, a web app that allows you to drag and drop in image files and define clickable areas that tie them together without needing to write code (http://www.invisionapp.com). Another app that works well for clickable demos is Axure (http://www.axure.com).

It does take more effort to assemble a demo than it does to throw together a slide deck. The benefit is that your audience is much less likely to zone out the way people do when they've seen too much PowerPoint. The demo

---

* For a good brief explanation of personas and how they are used in user research, see http://www.measuringusability.com/blog/personas-ux.php.

can also serve as lightweight product specs to illustrate a concept for the designers and developers who will be building the real thing.

The storytelling demo is the most conservative approach to customer development, and as such, the most limiting. Because you're giving your customers a clear picture to look at, you'll get feedback based on that demo as opposed to a higher-level look at their problems and current behaviors. Your customer is disproportionately likely to give positive feedback versus saying, "Actually, this doesn't solve a problem for me."

However, for companies that have never talked with customers in this manner and are stuck in a world of feature lists and data sheets, the storytelling demo is a great first step.

Incognito Customer Development

Sometimes you have more to worry about than customers reacting poorly to what you ask them about or show them. Your company's brand, market position, or current strategy may bias any conversations you might have.

The bias could be a halo effect: there's a large class of consumers who would rate any technology gadget higher if told it was made by Apple, for example. It may be a negative bias: imagine the same technology gadget, but branded as made by Walmart. This also affects companies that are trying to expand into a new industry or competency—you may love flying Southwest, but could you give objective feedback if they were talking to you about a prospective line of kitchen blenders?

Taking on a New Identity

When it's impossible for your company to have an untainted customer development conversation with your target customers, something needs to change. Either your company or your customer needs *to be someone else.*

Microsoft faced the problem of unavoidable bias when working on a total overhaul of Hotmail.com (now branded as Outlook.com). Once the leader in free email addresses, Hotmail had long been perceived as outdated, poorly designed, and even embarrassing.* Microsoft as a company suffered from a different problem: so many people use the Outlook email client in their workplace that they were likely to resist any changes to that familiar look and feel. Approaching potential customers as either Hotmail or

---

* Having a Hotmail or Yahoo! email address is enough to get you mocked publicly (*http://www. thedailybeast.com/galleries/2012/06/06/mitt-romney-s-hotmail-account-and-more-famous-people-with-outdated-email-providers-photos.html*).

But at least it's better than still using AOL mail (*http://theoatmeal.com/comics/email_address*).

Microsoft was unlikely to get objective feedback. Instead, Microsoft user researchers removed all traces of Microsoft from their conversations and prototypes. They used market research firms to recruit participants who met the target customer criteria, from cities across the United States. The researchers simply described themselves as being from a company working on ways to improve email and asked questions about the ways that customers were currently reading, composing, triaging, and sending email.

Conducting customer development without revealing your company affiliation doesn't need to be complicated. All you really need is a different domain name! If you contact people from an *@someplausibledomain.com* email address, it won't even occur to them that you may be from another company.

Talking to People Who Aren't Customers

Another way to do incognito customer development is to speak to people other than your current customers. While the best customer development interviews happen with your actual current or future customers, you can often learn a lot from the right proxies.

This may be a different stakeholder than your target customer, someone who lacks decision-making abilities but has a deep understanding of how things work in her particular environment—think administrative assistants, early-career product managers, or project managers. These people are easier to access, incredibly knowledgeable, and often underappreciated. You might even choose people from your own organization (if you haven't mined your customer support staff for insights, put this book down now and do it).

Depending on your business model, you may also have target customers who are users but not buyers. For example, think about an ad-supported service. While working on an online finance application, I didn't have access to the financial executives who were our target purchasers. But there was nothing stopping me from talking to *their* customers—the people who used their online banking and bill pay services.

Using Craigslist,* I was able to recruit a dozen online banking customers for interviews and a couple hundred for survey research.

---

* This anecdote dates back to 2005. Back then, using Craigslist to find survey participants worked beautifully; as I mentioned in Chapter 3, it's much less productive these days. If I were to repeat this exercise today with a budget, I would use a market research recruiting firm to find the appropriate customers. If I were to repeat this *without* a budget, I would probably start with interviewing friends and family. Everyone has to pay bills.

Through those interviews I learned how their banking customers were behaving and which online banking features they used. When we finally got the chance to pitch our target purchasers, we were able to say, "We've talked to your customers and we know what they need."

I learned that 88% of the customers I surveyed who had supposedly switched banks were still paying bills out of their old bank accounts because the process of setting up bill-pay information online was so tedious.

From the consumer perspective, this was merely a nuisance: they still had to carry two ATM cards and remember two PINs. For banks, it was a huge financial loss. Banks try to woo you to switch away from their competitor, but they don't make money just because you open a bank account: they make money when you keep most of your money with them. Banks want you to directly deposit your paycheck and then pay all of your bills from their account.

That opening guaranteed us a second meeting that we may not have otherwise gotten, and the insights from that research became a whole new product.

When multiple consumers told me the same problem, "I haven't switched my bill-pay account because it took me so long to set it up the first time," it was obvious that consumers and banks would benefit from a tool that automated the bill-pay account switchover. This insight became Yodlee BillPay Account Accelerator (*http://corporate.yodlee.com/solutions-payments-suite-yodlee-billpay.html*). While I am one of the joint patent holders for that product, I take no credit (or blame) for its horribly long name.

Show Me How You're Using Our Product

Incognito customer development is incredibly valuable for exploring new areas or new customer segments. But most people in larger, more mature companies are not looking for brand new products to create or new markets to tackle. You have a product; you need your customers to extract more value from it so that you can increase your revenue from your customers. You're not starting from scratch as an unknown. You need to work within your existing features and customer relationships.

When you have existing customers, they request features, report bugs, and complain to you or compliment you. You may be mistaking this communication for an understanding of how your customers behave and what they need. But you've probably also experienced frustration from building a feature or customization that a customer requested and then never used, or the confusion you feel when a seemingly happy customer cancels or doesn't come back.

How Can You Speed Up Innovation in a Large Company?

With a presence in all 50 states and over $50 billion in combined annualized revenue following its acquisition of Coventry Health Care this year, Aetna sits comfortably within the Fortune 100. That doesn't stop the company from actively looking for new ways to innovate and enter new markets. At the beginning of 2011, Aetna launched a new business unit—now called Healthagen—with the explicit mission of creating a portfolio of innovative businesses that deliver technologies and services to transform healthcare.

Since inception, the Healthagen Strategy Group has been innovating and incubating new businesses targeted at providers, payers, employers, and consumers. Early on the team recognized it needed to accelerate the incubation process to capture opportunities in the rapidly evolving healthcare market. "The opportunities for innovation are significant, but the traditional approaches and extensive due diligence involved in innovation were taking too long," says Hugh Ma, Head of Strategy for Healthagen. "We needed to move faster while minimizing risk."

Moving to lean

The inspiration for a new incubation approach occurred in mid-2012 after iTriage, a Healthagen portfolio company, hosted a successful hackathon. Charles Saunders, MD, CEO of Healthagen, saw the value of bringing together a diverse group of people with different skills and experiences to solve complex problems. He posed a question, "Could Healthagen use a hackathon approach for innovating business solutions to healthcare challenges?"

Hugh Ma and John Petito, former Strategy Lead, began developing a rapid business incubation approach leveraging their more than 25 years of combined experience in entrepreneurship, healthcare, strategy consulting, and technology. They concluded that concentrated, firsthand interaction with customers, users, and other stakeholders would validate needs as well as the product and market fit up front, and ultimately accelerate the process of building a new business. With inspiration from Steve Blank's *The Four Steps to the Epiphany* and Eric Ries's *The Lean Startup*, Ma and Petito developed a framework to place customer feedback front and center.

"Since the buyer and the consumer are often different people with different incentives, we needed real people in the conversation," explains Petito. The team created a rapid software development framework called SlingShot that would bring all parties together. By partnering customers and other relevant stakeholders with Healthagen entrepreneurs, product designers, and business experts, the team believed they could validate value propositions more quickly, identify potential barriers earlier, and avoid some traditional product development pitfalls. In essence, they compressed the early months, and even years, of a lean startup into a few months.

Rapid results

The time invested up front to understand needs and challenges across multiple stakeholders enabled the SlingShot team to develop specific hypotheses essential to the success of a business. Instead of showing slides or a demo during their SlingShot sessions, the team worked with Healthagen's internal designers to create materials and visuals to facilitate hypothesis-based conversations between the Healthagen team, customers, and consumers who would ultimately use the solutions. These immersion sessions provided a way to iterate in realtime and receive critical feedback. The early results spoke for themselves.

In the first event, the team went from a high-level idea to a business case, product visualizations, and customer advocates in four days. These results otherwise could have taken months and significantly greater investment.

In the second event, extensive multistakeholder collaboration led the team to identify an entirely new market previously unidentified by traditional approaches.

These results helped SlingShot to gain early momentum within Healthagen and Aetna as well as with potential customers. To facilitate broader adoption of lean principles across Healthagen and Aetna, Ma and Petito shared a SlingShot highlights video with everyone at Aetna and Healthagen by posting it on the company intranets. They also posted it on the Healthagen external website. Within six months, the Strategy team had a waiting list of teams across Healthagen and Aetna wanting to use SlingShot.

The current language of feature requests, voice-of-the-customer surveys, and 18-month product roadmaps just isn't broad enough to capture the value that your customers are currently getting or the opportunities that you're probably overlooking. If you want to know about those, you have to ask. And it feels a bit awkward.

As one account manager told me, "I've been working with these customers for almost a year. I can't ask about how they use our software *now*—it will seem like I haven't been paying attention all this time!" That's a very real fear, and here's a trick for getting around it: *Bring a new person into the mix*. You can then frame this conversation as "getting Bob up-to-speed with what's going on."

You'll need to see exactly what the customer is doing, either in person or via screen-sharing. If possible, visit the customer's home or office. You'll get to see the customer's physical location and the equipment she uses, not to mention the customer herself: her facial expressions, body language, and tone of voice (Figure 8-5).

Figure 8-5. Photos from Yammer site visits; it was a revelation to our team that our customers are trying to use Yammer to collaborate and work openly...while sitting in physically isolated cubicles

However, don't feel that you always need to do site visits. They require too much time and coordination to be practical for most people. You're better off using a lower-fidelity method more often. I often use conference calls with screen-sharing. Skype, Lync, and GoToMeeting all work well.

You'll want to start off with a brief explanation, but most of your conversation after that will be freeform:

> *As we've talked with our customers, one of the things we have found most valuable is to watch exactly how people are using our software. So I'd like for you to show me exactly what you do when you use our product. If there are times when you'd stop and do something else, or include someone else to help or see something, let me know as we go.*
>
> *How often do you typically use our software?*
>
> *What are you usually trying to accomplish when you start to use our software?*
>
> *OK, can you go ahead and start doing that task? Try to think out loud as you go, and describe what you're doing.*

Some customers will attempt to use this opportunity to request specific features ("see, this is why we need you to put X on the product roadmap"). Rather than debating, I've found it most useful to affirm, "Yes, I've written that down. Just to be clear for my notes, if you had feature X, can you repeat what that would allow you to do?" and then ask the customer to continue.

As the customer is walking through her usage, your job is to take notes and ask questions. You must refrain from offering your opinion or correcting what the customer is doing. If someone feels like she is making a mistake, or perceives that you are bored or impatient, she will stop acting naturally.

It's a balancing act: the more you talk, the less you will learn from your customer, but if you don't ask some prompting questions, you'll miss out on important insights. I recommend jotting down some notes about what you hope to learn in advance and then referring to them throughout your conversation. Here's an overview of what you should learn from these conversations:

How frequently customers are using your software (and how they are using it)

If you think customers are using your software daily and discover they are not, you need to figure out why. It may be that your software is lacking something, or worse, that it is not as valuable to the customer as you had assumed.

What your customer does immediately after using your software

Are they taking an action or making a decision based on what they do? Do they feel satisfied because they have successfully completed a task? (Or the opposite: I recently overheard someone in a coffee shop explain that she was taking a break because setting up an email campaign with her company's marketing automation software was so stressful that she always needed a break after using it.)

How your software aligns with your customer's workflow

Your suggested order of operations may conflict with existing processes or regulations. A process you assumed was completed by one person in one session may actually require multiple people or be broken into separate processes to stop and get explicit approval from a manager.

How much of your feature set is unused

Because customers often make buying decisions based on feature checklists, it's easy to assume that they use most or all of your functionality. I have never seen a customer who regularly uses more than 50% of the available functionality of any product I've worked on. This doesn't necessarily mean they are unhappy—if that small subset of features solves their problem, they may well be thrilled. It does mean that you may be heavily overinvesting in new features when you could be optimizing existing workflows.

New opportunities for you to provide value

Optimizing your default settings might save customers a few clicks and cut down on your support costs. Seeing which areas are confusing to customers might lead to a profitable professional services or training offering. Noticing that your customers export or import data to or from other programs might mean you should invest in integrations like embedded analytics or an improved API.

You may be concerned that this customer will expect you to fix all of the issues that she raised during this conversation. Perhaps surprisingly, this has never been my experience. Even difficult customers are often happier and easier to work with once you've invested time in listening to them.

Usage Frequency Versus Replaceability

At KISSmetrics, I remember talking to two customers back-to-back: the first told me eagerly that he opened up our analytics product every morning, first thing in the morning. The second customer admitted that he only used it once a week. My initial thought was that we were providing more value to the first customer.

However, as the interviews went on, it became clear that the first customer had only a surface-level understanding of the features. He was using the product, but had not incorporated it into any company-wide conversations or processes. Our product was easily replaceable.

The second customer was using KISSmetrics to set up and evaluate A/B tests. Reviewing results and incorporating them into the following week's sprint planning was a critical part of that customer's product development process.

Frequency of usage is often a good proxy for value and can be easily measured using quantitative analytics. However, when I have the opportunity to engage in conversations with customers, I like to probe a bit deeper to learn how replaceable our product is: how many people within a company or household use it or benefit from it? In what way is it used? Does it solve a single problem or multiple problems?

Replaceability—or the lack thereof—is an important qualitative metric to pursue.

Here's How to Use Our Product

Watching customers use your product is incredibly valuable—assuming that the customer knows how to use your product and is actively using it. What about brand new customers? Products with a steep learning curve?

Products with so much functionality that customers are using less than 10% of it? Customers who downloaded your app and tried it once, or subscription customers who've already canceled?

Instead of asking the customer how he uses your product, and then letting him drive the conversation, you can turn it around and be opinionated. Tell him, "Here's how you *should* be using our product..."

You may think that customers will not react well to being told what they should do. It actually works beautifully as long as you explain what you're doing in advance. Make it clear that you are relying on the customer to correct you when your assumptions are wrong:

> As we're trying to improve this product, one of the most difficult challenges is that we can only assume how it fits with our customers' goals and processes.
>
> I'd like to walk through how we envision someone like you using this product, based on what we've learned from other customers. Please interrupt me when I get things wrong and when you disagree with my assumptions—and I know that will happen. Also please feel free to ask me questions as I go.

After you make the first assertion—something as simple as "I assume you would use this product twice a week"—pause, and then deliberately ask the interviewee to agree or disagree. This makes it clear that you *want* him to interrupt, as opposed to silently agreeing to be polite.

For this exercise, you'll want to be as opinionated as possible. The more direct you are, the easier it is for the interviewee to agree or disagree with you. If you say, "you could use option A, B, C, or D," he probably agrees with at least one of those choices. If you say "You should use A," then it's easier for him to say, "Actually, can you explain B? That sounds more like what my company would use."

Because you are doing most of the talking, you will learn less from this approach than you would from a more open-ended exercise. However, if you are early in the process of exploring a new idea, this is a good way to validate or invalidate some of your assumptions.

Some of the things you can learn from this style of interview include:

Identifying restrictions

Legal or regulatory restrictions, existing processes, and resource limitations are often obvious to your interviewee, even if she doesn't understand the details of your idea or product yet.

Clarity of your value proposition

If you assert that customers should perform a certain task, they should immediately understand its value. If you try to explain why and they still seem confused, your value proposition is either unclear or it's not actually valuable to them.

Why unused features are unused

As you explain a specific feature, ask if the interviewee had noticed it and what he thinks it does. His response can reveal whether you should fix an interface element to make a feature more discoverable, fix some text labeling to make it clearer, or drop the feature because it is not solving problems for the customer.

Because you are explaining how to use the product, you can use this method as both training and research. While at KISSmetrics, I would often conduct this type of opinionated walkthrough with brand-new customers. The customer considered it a service, and I learned about different companies' processes and constraints.

Later Is Better than Never

Throughout this book, I've emphasized the importance of getting concepts in front of customers as early as possible. But there are situations when it is disadvantageous, or even impossible, to get customer input early in the process.

"Kinect was an impossible product," says Ben Smith, Program Manager at Microsoft Xbox, "but all innovation comes out of impossibility. It was a 36-month project that we launched in 19 months."

When the Xbox team proposed Kinect, they were taking a big chance. Investing in Kinect would mean postponing major innovations to the existing Xbox platform. And because of the need for secrecy, the team had limited ability to validate the customer risk early in the product development process. They had to trust their intuition, internal domain expertise, and product vision: to build something "as fun to watch as it is to play."

Validate assumptions using lean startup principles

But even without the early ability to talk to customers, the Kinect team was able to reduce risk and systematically validate assumptions using lean startup principles. "We had incubation on one path and product development on another," explains Smith. "The people who work in our incubators are the ones who think, 'What could happen if these 95 impossible things were to line up?' and then they learn just enough about those things to start building something out that approximates a prototype. They think about all the approaches we could take and say, 'Let's start building them, one after another.' "

The team brainstormed huge lists of questions. How much latency would customers find acceptable? How would they get the needed motion-capture information? What software and hardware optimizations were possible? They also identified risks and actively sought to reduce them. For example, the Kinect was built using entirely off-the-shelf parts so they wouldn't be beholden to custom suppliers. The team built temporary motion-capture stages on the basketball courts on the Microsoft campus, to get that data faster and quicker. (Later, upon discovering that building a permanent stage for motion capture required waiting months for building permits, the team rented one instead.)

To maintain focus, the team moved from a Waterfall development methodology to Agile—with two-week sprints broken down into one-day deliverables. "Every night at 6 p.m., we'd get in a room and ask each other, 'What questions did you answer today?'"

Try out prototypes

A year into development, the Kinect team was finally able to get early prototypes into the hands of real customers. As soon as the Kinect prototype was able to do a simple monkey-see, monkey-do, where the player could move and see his bare-bones avatar moving on the screen, the team started bringing in people.

"The first surprising thing that hit us is that the technology inside Kinect is invisible. There's nothing to hold; there's no vibration or haptic feedback. So players would just sit in front of it and wait for something to happen!"

The team had to invent ways to help players feel successful right away and also to have things fail in a way where players could quickly fix the situation.

The team arranged with Macy's for 12 store locations where anyone could play Kinect on Saturday mornings. This served two purposes: it helped the team gather a more diverse collection of skeletal motion-capture data,* and it allowed them to observe real customers interacting with the Kinect in a casual, social setting. "We are the worst judges of our own products," says Smith. "We had to construct a beta program. We had to measure living rooms. Seeing how real people use your stuff versus how you assumed or wanted them to use it—that's critically important. It would have been a massive failure if we hadn't constantly gotten new and diverse people in front of the interface."

Xbox One shipped in December 2013 with an updated version of Kinect.

---

* As Smith recounts, "Up until this point, most of the skeleton motion capture data we'd collected was from employees. This being Microsoft, that meant we had mostly data from Caucasian, slightly overweight men."

It Can Work For You, Too

Now that you've read through these customer development techniques, you should feel ready to start using customer development to validate your upcoming features, product releases, and new initiatives. While large companies may have to pay some additional "tax" in terms of clearly setting expectations, choosing customers carefully, and producing higher-quality mockups or feature releases, there is nothing about existing companies, products, and customers that is incompatible with forming and validating hypotheses.

You may think that there's one topic that I didn't cover: time. In a small company or startup, there is far more freedom to take a week or two to dive into customer development. But in a larger company, there are often preset release dates, promises to customers, and, more importantly, dozens or even hundreds of employees who can't sit around waiting for the results of an extended customer development effort. What you learn from customers has to happen in parallel with your existing product development processes, and it has to happen fast.

In the next chapter, I'll talk about ways to fit customer development tactics into existing customer touchpoints. You'll learn how to take advantage of fast customer development techniques that are light on process and that anyone in your company can use.

Key Takeaways

- If you have an existing product and customers, adapt the MVP concept.

- Being a recognized brand may bias prospective customers. You can practice "incognito customer development" by using a different domain, or rough, unbranded sketches.

- Make it more viable than minimum, but make sure it doesn't go far beyond minimum.

- Find the customers who would be very disappointed if they couldn't use your product anymore.

- When doing customer development with existing customers, overcommunicate that you are asking questions, not building something.

- Use the storytelling demo to explain to the customer how a fictional person uses your product.

- Ask customers to show you how they use your product.

- Show the customer how to use your product and be didactic to encourage them to disagree with you.

CHAPTER 9

Ongoing Customer Development

The beautiful part is that it's not hard to find sports fans and people who love to talk about sports! If I'm on an airplane and I look across the aisle, so often I see someone using ESPN. I'll turn to them and just start talking: "What do you like about the site? What else do you wish you could do?"

—Ryan Spoon, Senior Vice President of Product Development, ESPN

You need to stop thinking of customer support as a crew of responsive hole-patchers that deal with problems as they come up, but instead as investigators who have privileged access to the information that holds the key to the future of your business: customer insights.

—Dan Martell, CEO of Clarity

Many companies struggle to incorporate ongoing customer development research into their product development process. Where does it fit, and how will we find the time?

At the beginning of a new project, it's (relatively) easy to justify dedicated time and resources for learning about customers. But when product development is ongoing and iterative, customer development research must be as well. If we wait until we have a chunk of time to devote to customer research, it will never happen.

Luckily, ongoing customer development doesn't need to involve forming hypotheses or finding time to fit in 20 hours of interviews. It doesn't have to be planned and scheduled.

In this chapter, we'll talk about how companies with existing products and customers can incorporate customer development into their day-to-day processes. Startups, these methods will work for you too, although you'll find that some of the details (working with people with specific job roles, dealing with cross-functional communication issues, and justifying why customer development is beneficial) are less applicable to your organizations.

We'll talk about:

- Getting help from people who are already talking to customers

- Taking advantage of customer-initiated interactions

- Getting below the surface when customers request features

We'll also talk about how to bring all of the feedback together so that everyone in your organization can be smarter about what customers need and how your organization is responding. Don't skip this closing-the-loop step—it takes time, but it keeps your team engaged and motivated.

With these methods, you won't need to wait until you can set aside time. You'll be equipped to turn any conversation into a question that allows you to constantly learn about your customers, five minutes at a time.

Who's Already Out of the Building?

Of course it's a great idea to do a little customer development any time you meet a customer, but tactically, you may still be wondering: when am I going to get the chance to ask customers a question apart from my interviews? Change your thinking here: the more appropriate question here is not when but who.

News flash: There are people in your company who talk to customers every day.

They may not be familiar with customer development or lean startup principles, but they're perfectly positioned to listen and learn. There's incredible potential to learn if you harness the power of your customer-facing coworkers.

Salespeople, account managers, and customer support professionals spend their entire work lives talking with your prospective and current customers. Unfortunately, what these customer-facing folks learn is too often dismissed by people who make product decisions. "She'll promise anything to close the deal." "He's just hearing from a skewed sample of angry customers."

Sure, there's bias. But that doesn't mean we should ignore this feedback; it means we try to reduce the bias.

Here's what typically happens:

> **Sales:** *Big Customer won't sign the contract unless we build an additional security widget.*

> **Product management:** *We can't build that; it would only benefit Big Customer and we've got a ton of higher-priority features in our backlog.*

> *Sales goes back to the customer and tells him no, possibly losing the deal. Sales blames product management for being short-sighted while product management rolls its eyes at another idiotic request from sales. Meanwhile, no one understands why Big Customer wanted that security widget in the first place.*

Instead, these teams can work together to produce a better outcome for both. When a customer asks for a feature or demands a change, the best answer is not "yes" or "no." Each of those answers signals an end to the conversation. Asking questions in response is a more diplomatic way of avoiding a no as well as a valuable means of getting answers.

At Yammer, I give a training session as part of the onboarding process for new salespeople and account managers, to offer examples of this type of conversational technique:

> **Customer:** *We can't buy until we have your assurance that you'll build an additional feature X.*

> **Sales:** *I'd like to make sure I fully understand your needs so that I can bring this feedback back to our product team. Can I ask you a couple of questions about feature X and how it would help you and your company?*

> **Customer:** *I'm hearing lots of complaints from our internal employees who use the product because you haven't built feature Y.*

> **Account manager:** *It sounds like you're hearing from some unhappy people. I want to be sure I'm clear on the issue—can I ask more about the context? What are employees trying to accomplish that they are unable to do? If they had feature Y, how would they expect to use it?*

The customer provides more details, which helps the salesperson to figure out whether this is a real need or a bluff to get a discount. The customer appreciates that the salesperson is trying to understand his needs as opposed to just closing a deal. The product team potentially learns about some hidden need or constraint that they may want to address.

New sales and account managers are often skeptical that this will work. They suspect, rightfully, that customers will not respond well to being asked why they want something.

Asking why does require some linguistic softening. Prefacing why questions with some polite phrasing makes them sound more conversational and less interrogative. For more details, see "Be Diplomatic with Why?" in Chapter 5.

In some organizations, the relationship between product development and sales may be strained. If that's the case, it may not be realistic to say, *"Hey—on your sales calls, I want you to do research for me!"*

I've been in that situation, and what worked for me was to focus more on my coworkers' needs than on the research aspect. I've said something like this:

> *I know it can be challenging for you when you're trying to close a deal and customers are asking for features and you can't promise them.*
>
> *Even though I can't say yes, I don't want to put you in the position where you have to tell them no. Can I suggest responding to them with a question? In the worst case scenario, it gives you a more positive spin on the conversation—but hopefully it also allows you to learn something more about them that will help you build the relationship.*

Volunteering to help out with sales calls or account maintenance visits are also good ways to repair relationships and demonstrate customer development. Seeing it in action is the best way to get someone on your side.

Palantir, a company that develops data analysis software for intelligence agencies and the military, takes it one step further and removes the middleman. Instead of training salespeople to listen to customers, they send engineers into the field:

> *These techies don't create the company's products—at least, not at first. They're out in the field, interacting directly with customers and making sure the product is meeting their needs.... They can tackle the customer's problems on the spot—and, most important, begin to identify new problems the client might not know it has.* *

---

* *To Sell is Human: The Surprising Truth About Moving Others* by Daniel Pink, p. 34.

Who Can It Be, Knocking at Your Door?

Customer support is not just a cost to make problems go away; it's a listening post. —Darius Dunlap

People often use the excuse that they can't do customer development because their customers would find it intrusive. That may be a legitimate reason not to call a Fortune 500 CEO on her cell and ask for a 20-minute interview, but if you have customers using and paying for your products, you already have opportunities every single day when they contact you: customer support.*

Good customer support professionals are an amazingly underutilized resource. No one knows a product better than the person who has to answer questions and file bugs against it all day long.

We Didn't Know Who We Were Building For

When she started working in customer support for Mindbody, a company that offers studio-management software, Vanessa Pfafflin kept hearing the same questions. "Easy questions, like 'How do I cancel a class?' or 'How do I void a sale?' but after a while I realized that we could fix the underlying problems. I started writing down customer quotes and taking screenshots and adding quick suggestions for how to fix the user interface so customers wouldn't have these questions in the first place," she says.

When business surged one month, everyone had to help staff the support lines—including the CEO. He was surprised by how many customers were having difficulty with the most basic, commonly used features, and asked Pfafflin to work on identifying and reducing problems *before* they happened.

---

* Apologies to Men at Work for the title of this section. I don't advise taking the tactic of the song's narrator, though I do know plenty of companies that would prefer to "run and hide" from users offering feedback.

"I studied the tech support logs to find the most frequent problems, and then proposed solutions. One screen was our number one source of calls—a task that all customers had to use frequently to set prices for their services. It was complicated—a total nightmare. We ran some queries and determined that the average customer only used 4 of 15 options. We hid the other 11 choices behind an Advanced Settings link and call volume dropped dramatically. If we'd talked with our customers earlier, we might have realized we didn't need to build those options at all."

When Mindbody brought in usability researcher Jared Spool to consult, he encouraged the team to do field research. "Jared told us we had no idea who we were building for," says Pfafflin. "And he was right. No one talked to customers except for the support staff, and that team didn't talk to the engineers."

Pfafflin became the company's first user researcher. She introduced regular site visits, bringing engineers and designers to customer offices to watch people use the product. "We saw people make mistakes that they weren't even calling us to complain about. They were the types of mistakes that a customer would forget to mention because when she's using our product, the studio is bustling and full of customers. Or they'd blame themselves, thinking they were making a mistake."

Mindbody started requiring everyone who had their hands on the product to observe the customer for two hours every six weeks. They could go on a site visit, listen in on a sales call, or sit in on user research. "And at first people complained! But when someone sees a customer struggling, and then has the ability to submit a solution and implement it, that was really rewarding to our whole team."

Feature requests and complaints can be the most frustrating types of interactions for a support professional. He's responding to a customer who is often already angry, and he has no fix or timeline to promise.

The surprising truth is that questions are an extremely effective tool for defusing negativity. When you ask a follow-up question, the customer feels heard and understood. Questions signal a partnership: let's fix this. Even a customer who comes to you furious has a hard time staying angry when the person on the phone is actively seeking to understand his problem and fix it. Darius Dunlap, founder of SupportUX Consulting, jokes that, "You actively listen to the customer and all of a sudden, he's in his mind switching from thinking 'They're idiots' to 'Wow, they're actually thinking about this.'"

Feature Requests

For feature requests, a good format is to restate the customer's description and then ask why he wants it. Restating the customer's words ensures that you understand him correctly. It also softens the impact of the "why?" question, helping you sound curious rather than accusatory:

> *To make sure I understand you correctly: you're saying that you want us to add a data export feature?*

> *If we built this data export feature, what would you be able to do that you aren't able to do today?*

Response rates to this type of question are extremely high because the customer believes that answering will increase the odds of getting the desired feature. Rachel Pennig, Director of Customer Support for Recurly, explains, "We say to customers, 'Tell us everything you need to be able to do, and we're not always going to be able to say yes but we can pass it along and use your feedback to make informed decisions.' I recently talked with a customer who wanted a way to create sixty thousand billing plans! By asking what he was trying to accomplish, I was able to come up with a reasonable solution using three plans."

Listen…But Don't Take Customer Suggestions at Face Value

Two things that never fail to surprise me (Figure 9-1):

- That 20 customers can make what sounds like the same request. When you talk to them to learn more, they're actually each trying to solve *different* problems. At Yammer, customers frequently suggest greater administrative controls as a desired enhancement. That means entirely different things to each customer.

- That 20 customers can suggest different features or changes, but when you talk to them to learn more, they're all experiencing the same underlying problem. At KISSmetrics, we built version 1.0 of our analytics debugger that customers relied upon heavily. Each customer proposed different solutions for how to improve the tool, but all of them stemmed from the same issues around information display and density.

One suggestion,
many underlying problems

Many suggestions,
same underlying problem

*Figure 9-1. Customers tend to make suggestions rather
than talk about the problems they're facing, which adds
a layer of abstraction that you need to push beyond*

Functionality or Design Issues

Functionality or interface complaints require a bit more deliberate politeness. At KISSmetrics, my guidelines for customer support included 4 As
(apologize, admit, ask, appreciate).* Apologizing for the customer's bad experience and admitting blame sets the right tone for asking questions—you
don't want to inadvertently imply that the customer is at fault. An email
reply might look like this:

> *I'm sorry—the date selector widget is not an intuitive experi-
> ence right now. We should explain in the inline text when the next
> month's report will be available.*
>
> *May I ask you a question? I'd like to understand your use case more
> clearly. Do you use this feature around the same time each month?
> Are you the only person who uses it, or do other people in different
> job roles use it?*
>
> *Thank you for reaching out to us; we are always trying to improve
> the product experience and your input is incredibly helpful.*

What you can expect to learn from these responses are important details:
who is affected by a problem, under what circumstances it occurs, how
often it occurs, and how severe the problem is.

In many cases, interactions may have tested well in standard usability
testing but don't align with someone's existing behavior patterns. For
these types of problems, for every one complaint, there are often 10 more

---

* *http://www.cindyalvarez.com/communication/the-4-as-of-responding-to-customer-criticism*

customers suffering in silence (or groaning in frustration) while they think about switching to a different product or service.

Bugs and Errors

When a customer first comes to support with a bug report or error that needs fixing, customer development should not be top of mind. The first priority is to address the concern and resolve the customer's issue. However, anyone who has worked in customer support knows that answering the question that your customer asked is not always the same as answering the question that your customer *should have* asked. Support professionals are probably already familiar with the art of gracefully transitioning from giving an answer and then asking an additional question:

> *Can I ask what task you're trying to accomplish when you use this functionality? I'm asking because I want to make sure that I've given you the most useful answer possible. If there's an easier or better way to do what you need to do, I want to make sure I get you that solution.*

Once you've provided an answer, you've got a captive audience, and you may as well use it!

Aside from phone and email support, many web-based products use live chat to answer questions for customers and sales leads. When a customer initiates a question, that's a good opportunity to identify her pain point and ask some additional questions. You'll have closer to 2 minutes than 20, but that's still enough time to learn something.

Question of the Week

Perhaps you don't have a specific customer development question or a graceful way to fit one into the conversation.

Not all questions have to be specific to your customers' experiences. There's a lot of useful background research that you can answer from simple, survey-format questions.

The easiest way to do this is to pick a standard question each week on some topic that you'd like to learn more about. When I answered customer support emails for KISSmetrics, I often manually added a question to the bottom, which only took a few seconds:

If you have additional questions, or I didn't fully resolve your issue, please let me know.

Since we're always eager to learn more about our customers, I'd like to ask you one more (unrelated) question:

How many hours this past week did you spend in meetings?

If you use a support ticketing system, it should be easy to export and search for the answers to this question.

The best generic questions are ones with factual answers that are either numerical or answer who/what/how/when/why. It takes longer for the customer to write the answer to a subjective question, and those answers tend to be less useful if you're not following up on them with more questions.

Recognizing Bias

The people who initiate interactions with you are probably not a representative sample. The silent majority is an apt term for the bulk of your customers who neither complain nor compliment.

When I worked at Yodlee, support requests and posts to our customer forums were heavily skewed toward people with a high degree of technical literacy and financial domain knowledge. They were constantly seeking to push the limits of how our products could be used. At KISSmetrics, I split my time between absolute beginners and experts (who knew far more about web analytics than I did!). At Yammer, many of our support and feature requests are funneled through a community manager or project manager.

Luckily, there is probably consistency in the type of person who reaches out to you. Once you recognize the direction toward which feedback is biased, you can correct accordingly. When power users or proxy customers such as admins or managers offer feedback, it's a good idea to investigate how many users it impacts. It's not uncommon for power users to clamor for improvements to a feature that 90% of users have never even tried. When extremely low-tech or inexperienced customers offer feedback, it's worth evaluating whether they are viable customers or whether their inexperience is too high a barrier to getting value from your product.

Closing the Loop

How do you ensure that all of the great information that different teams are learning doesn't get lost in the shuffle?

I strongly recommend starting with as little formal process as possible. Closing the loop is important, so to ensure that you keep doing it, you'll need to make it extremely easy on participants and on you.

Closing the loop has three components: collecting information, summarizing it (as described in Chapter 6), and sharing an appropriate level of detail to inform without overwhelming. With incremental customer development, we aren't always seeking to invalidate a specific hypothesis but rather to keep learning as our product and customers change over time. The notes from incremental customer development are often a jumping-off point for forming a new hypothesis, doing some more in-depth usability research, or digging into our analytics data.

Collecting Information

How you collect customer development notes from other people should depend on the tools that your company is already using. If it takes multiple clicks or written instructions to submit notes, people won't take the time. What's the easiest, most lightweight way for people to communicate currently? Here are some methods I've seen for getting people who talk to customers to give you customer development input themselves:

- Shared Word or Google Doc where anyone can paste in notes
- Shared Evernote or OneNote notebook where anyone can paste in notes
- Separate email address that anyone can forward emails or notes to
- Google Form that submits notes to a spreadsheet

At KISSmetrics, I used the Google Form approach. I added the default recommended questions or prompts with a freeform text area for responses, and then added an extra Other question at the end. This allowed the interviewer to bookmark a link to the form, take notes directly into the form, and then quickly click Submit at the end. This approach had two big benefits: I didn't have to nag my coworkers to get their notes, and it was easy to do a quick follow-up after their very first form submission to offer some light feedback or suggest a prompt or follow-up question for the next time.

However, what works best is what gets you the most useful information. In many organizations it may be more effective to just call your coworkers to find out what they learned. Customer-facing employees may be traveling and having face-to-face conversations instead of carrying a notebook or sitting in front of a computer, so all of their notes live in their heads.

Sharing the Impact of Customer Development

Your goal is to make smart product decisions based on what you've learned about your customers' problems and needs. When you do that, you need to share that explicitly back to your organization. Don't assume that people will understand how customer development has had an impact! (Remember that people practicing customer development are focusing on problems; they may not recognize the solutions that you end up choosing as a result of those problems.)

When customer development saves time or money, helps avoid a mistake, or dramatically increases a customer's satisfaction, that's a win to be celebrated:

> *We learned _____*
>
> *So we didn't build [feature/partnership/new product]*
>
> *Which saved us ____ time!*

As you may remember from the Preface, the interviews I conducted in my first month at KISSmetrics allowed us to cut back our product development scope dramatically. We saved at least two months of development time as well as the ongoing cost of supporting overly complex code.

Here's a more subtle way to state results:

> *We learned _____*
>
> *So we tried _____*
>
> *Which resulted in _____ positive metrics change!*

Success stories like this fit well on a slide, but for maximum impact, don't just share them in a meeting. Print out summaries like this on posters and stick them on the walls. At Yammer, we often have short summaries of customer learnings either taped to the wall or showing on the ambient TV displays in the office. That helps everyone—not just the people at one meeting—view customer development as part of the company's culture.

Whether you share stories like this weekly, monthly, or randomly as you have a story to tell depends on the pace of your organization and how much input you're getting. In a small startup, weekly feels right. In a larger organization, a weekly customer development success update may feel like overloading people's inboxes.

At Yammer, our user research team shares updates at a monthly internal all-hands meeting. We also share our insights with the customers themselves once a quarter with our private community of enterprise Yammer customers, and sometimes even on our public-facing blog. We try to summarize information as "Here's what we learned from you and here's what we've done as a result." Our customers don't always agree with our solutions, but the transparency into how we learn and prioritize promotes great questions and challenges from them. In other words, talking about customer development is actually another way to practice customer development.

Now You're Ready

In the past nine chapters, you've learned to reframe your thinking, form hypotheses, and find customers to talk with. We've walked through interviewing, analyzing, and turning your notes into actionable product decisions.

My hope is that many of you didn't actually make it to this point by reading straight through—that you set the book down, called a customer, and learned about what problems she was trying to solve. I hope you have already invalidated a few assumptions, formed some new hypotheses, and figured out additional questions to ask.

You'll find that customer development gets easier and feels more natural with each interview. You'll make mistakes—I'd be disappointed if you didn't—but they'll be fast and provide learning to make your next attempt more effective.

Along the way, if you have questions, I'd love to hear from you. I'll be continuing to collect blog posts, templates, and success stories at *http://www. leancustomerdevelopment.com*. You can also always reach me at *cindy@ leancustomerdevelopment.com*. Good luck!

Key Takeaways

- Teach everyone who talks to customers easy ways to participate in customer development.

- When customers make feature requests, ask them what they could do if they had that feature that they can't do today.

- To understand what customers value, ask your most active or enthusiastic customers to describe your product to someone else.

- Share customer development successes with your organization, showing how things you've learned from customers made a positive change.

- The best signals about what's wrong come from customer support.

- By asking an angry customer a question and listening, you can learn more about their problem. Listening is conciliatory for the customer and learning for you.

- Why you need to ask questions to find out about the real problem: customers make different suggestions to solve the same underlying problem. Many customers may offer similar suggestions, but have different underlying problems.

- Add an extra question to your email messages to customers. Frame it so you can tally the results.

Questions That Work

Customer development doesn't always have to be scheduled, or part of a structured interaction.

Trying to craft an effective question while you're carrying on a conversation can be challenging. It's easy to inadvertently ask a leading question (How often do you think you would use X?) or a yes-or-no question that elicits a one-word response (Do you think Y is a good lunch option for your family?). Yes-or-no questions are not only ineffective, but they throw the ball right back in your court since they do not elicit a more open-ended response. You have to have another question ready immediately. Since you want to listen more than you talk, that's not a good strategy.

In this appendix, I give you a list of questions you can use. For each question, we'll talk about how the question is constructed, when it makes sense to ask it, and what you can learn by asking it.

WARNING —————————————————————————

Do not ask questions that you could have answered yourself using a search engine. People enjoy feeling helpful by providing information that is specific to them. Treat them as experts, not research assistants.*

---

* Don't ask someone when her industry's annual conference is or ask for a list of schools in her city—those are facts that you should be willing to look up on your own. Don't ask for information that you could find if you read her corporate website or watched her marketing videos. The Let Me Google That for You website was created to reflect this feeling of insulted indignation. From their About text: "This is for all the people who find it more convenient to bother you with their question rather than google it for themselves" (*http://www.lmgtfy.com*).

Questions for Any Customer Development Interview

Whether you work for a startup or an established company, these questions can help you.

Tell me about the last time you ____

The situation

> The customer is talking about a specific task, either complaining about it or expressing the wish to do it faster, better, or not at all.
>
> This isn't a question as much as an invitation to speak freely. It doesn't make sense to ask questions that measure time, effort, cost, or value because you don't yet know whether any of those attributes are interesting.
>
> Another important feature of this question is that you're asking about a tangible past action, not a potential future action. When people talk about things they may do in the future, they tend to be more aspirational, more positive, and less accurate.

What you'll learn

> When you don't imply that you're looking for a specific type of information, the customer will simply talk about what is most significant to her about that task. It may be related to who, what, why, when, or how; it may be a positive or negative emotion.

NOTE

What the customer chooses to talk about first is a guide to how you should continue the conversation.

If you could wave a magic wand and change anything about how you [perform this task], what would it be?

The situation

> This question is an effective way to help a customer who is fixated on a specific solution or hampered by a real or perceived limitation.

What you'll learn

> This question forces customers to identify their biggest pain point. It's often a way to learn more about a customer's environment: would his magic wand help him do something faster or better, or eliminate obstacles or bureaucracy?

What tools do you use for _____?

The situation

This question elicits specifics. It helps to prompt a customer to move beyond generalized descriptions of how he completes a task or deals with a situation.

Even when you have made it clear that you are interested in a customer's specific experiences, she doesn't always believe you: "Oh, I didn't think you wanted me to mention individual websites or apps that I use—I figured you'd want a general answer that might apply to other people too."

What you'll learn

Specific websites, equipment, software programs, apps, or methods that the customer uses. If the customer is using tools to try and solve a problem, that's a good sign. It shows that she recognizes the problem and is already committed to trying to solve it. (A customer who intends to try a solution to a problem but hasn't gotten around to it yet is usually a red herring.)

When you started using [tool], what benefit were you expecting?

The situation

Use this question if the customer thinks his problem is solved. He's using a product that at least partially addresses his pain points. He may not be actively seeking a better solution.

What you'll learn

The customer's initial expectations around solving his problem. If the tool is a commercial product (as opposed to something like pencil and paper), it's useful to look at that product's marketing. Compare the value promised by the product's marketing with the customer's expectations.

The whole problem may not be solved

It's common for customers to start using a product or service for one purpose and then discover it's useful for a different purpose. The customer may be completely satisfied with the product's new value but still have an unsolved problem. A good follow-up question is:

Is there anything you expected to be able to do with [tool name] that you aren't able to?

How often do you do _____? Let's say, how many times in the past month?

The situation

Usually I find myself asking this question when the customer has expressed interest in a product or feature to help her solve a problem with a task or routine.

"How often" sounds appropriately conversational so it doesn't put the person on the defensive. Since people tend to be bad at estimating the frequency of events, following it up with a specific window of time in the past (not too long a window; here I used a month) makes it easier for them to give you an accurate count. Using a "how many times" framing is also helpful if you are asking about behaviors that are less socially acceptable or that the customer is embarrassed about.*

What you'll learn

Obviously, you're asking how often a situation occurs, which helps you figure out whether this is a significant enough problem to invest in solving.

You're also implicitly asking about priority. It's not uncommon for someone to describe a situation that happens all the time and then admit that it hasn't happened in the past month. How does the customer then react? Does she laugh and admit that, "OK, maybe it's not that big a deal after all," or does she say defensively, "Well, it *seems* like it happens all the time." The latter is a clue that this is a particularly severe problem or one that causes constant low-level stress. That's a problem worth looking into!

When this occurs, how much additional time or money does it cost you or your company?

The situation

You've identified a problem but you're not sure if you can fix it profitably. This question is also helpful if you're uncertain of the severity of the customer's pain point because the customer is not showing much

---

* One of my friends is a nurse practitioner for a free clinic in a low-income urban neighborhood. She was trained to ask "How often have you used drugs in the past week?" instead of "Do you use drugs?" because patients respond (more or less) honestly to the first question and lie in response to the second one. Without an accurate picture of the patient's habits, it's more difficult to provide effective medical care.

emotion. (Of course, in a public space such as a conference or sales meeting, people tend to exhibit more reserved emotional responses.)

What you'll learn

How this customer thinks about time and money. Is he the one responsible for budgeting either of them? Is this customer the primary user of your product but not the person who makes a purchasing decision?

Helping them quantify

Many people (especially consumers but also businesspeople) are not accustomed to quantifying time or money wasted. People make a lot of irrational decisions. However, it's useful to guide a customer through this calculation:

Interviewer: *You just described a problem that happens in your household, realizing that you've run out of groceries. When this occurs, how much additional time or money is it costing you?*

Customer: *Well, I just run to the store, or maybe call for a pizza.*

Interviewer: *So, if you make an unplanned trip to the grocery store, how long does that take?*

Customer: *Oh…maybe 20 minutes. Well, 30, if it's crowded in the store.*

Interviewer: *How is the rest of your night affected, taking that extra 30 minutes to get to the store and shop and come back?*

Customer: *Well, then we're eating dinner later, so there's a rush to get the kids' homework done and then bath and bedtimes go late. That's why it's tempting to just order a pizza.*

Interviewer: *How does the cost of pizza for dinner compare to what you would have cooked if there were groceries?*

Your goal is not to get to a precise dollars and cents (or hours and minutes) calculation, but to get a more concrete sense of the value you're providing.

Who else experiences this problem?

The situation

You're looking for additional segments of customers to target, or you're not sure if your initial target customer profile is accurate.

What you'll learn

Who else you could be talking to. Another benefit to this question is that your customer may have a better sense than you of what he has in common with other customers. For example, if you were building a product for babies, you might assume that your target customers are parents. But parents know that they are not the only purchasers of baby things—buyers include grandparents, doting aunts, neighbors, and anyone invited to a baby shower. A more accurate target customer description may be people who buy presents for babies.

When you do (or use) _____, is there anything you do immediately before to prepare?

The situation

You can always ask this question—almost any task or routine includes preparation steps that we don't always think about. This is also a useful ice-breaker question when you're talking to a customer who doesn't seem to have anything to complain about, such as an existing customer who has fallen into a routine. Nothing is explicitly broken, so she doesn't think about what could be improved. Or perhaps you asked the "tell me about how you ____" question and you sense that the customer's answer was too narrow in scope.

What you'll learn

There may be existing preconditions required for the customer to use your product (I only use X when I'm on a business trip). If there are related activities or tasks that someone always does before using your product, that's an opportunity to extend your feature set or partner with a complementary product or service.

Online bill pay is surprisingly manual

When I was at Yodlee, my design team partnered with a major consumer bank to figure out how to create a significantly better online bill-pay experience. The project was canceled before engineering resources were committed, but I've never forgotten a surprising insight that I kept hearing from the customers I interviewed:

Customer: *I don't have any real complaints about using online bill pay—it just works, and it's more convenient than writing checks and remembering to get stamps.*

Me: *You told me about the steps you go through when you pay your bills online. Is there anything that you do before you come to the bank's website to prepare?*

Customer: *No... well, I know the bank shows me my balance, but that's not accurate because I'm going to get money from the ATM between now and when these bills are due. And I have a couple of* *bills that automatically debit. So I need to figure out what's going to really be left.*

Me: *How do you do that?*

Customer: *I usually grab some scratch paper and a pen and just subtract, you know, I have this much money, and then subtract what I think I'm going to withdraw, and then subtract the auto debit amounts. Then I know what my real balance is going to be and I can start filling in the amounts I want to pay online.*

This customer defined paying her bills online as going to the website, but it actually included this preparatory offline step. I heard variations of this story from multiple people!

Now, would it make business sense to build an additional calculator tool into an online banking website? Maybe not; banks do make an awful lot of their revenue from customers who accidentally overdraft their accounts. As someone who'd been designing financial software for years, it was amazing to me to discover this common user behavior that I had no idea existed.

Here's a related question:

When you do (or use) _____, is there anything that you do immediately afterward?

Similar to the question above, this is a good way to learn more about a situation from a wider angle. I talked in Chapter 4 about abstracting up a level when you ask questions—asking what people do before and after a specific task or habit is another way of doing that.

Would you be willing to help us by participating in user research or beta testing?

The situation

Always ask this question at the end of every interview! Don't wait until you have a formal beta testing program in place. It's extremely useful to have a bank of email addresses of people who've already agreed to help you out in the future.

What you'll learn

If you're solving customer problems, people will say yes to this question. If you get a lot of "no" answers, view that as invalidating your hypothesis.

How asking this question helps with future product development

Once you have people willing to answer questions, you can cut down dramatically on the number of assumptions that your team has to make in future product development. You can quickly take simple assertions (I assume most of our customers are using this feature while they're traveling) and send them to a handful of people via email for feedback:

> *Quick question: Is there a specific occasion or situation occurring when you're using [feature]? (If so, what is it?)*

> *We'd like to make sure we understand how people are using [feature] before we decide which changes to prioritize. Thanks for your help!*

It's worth taking a moment to wordsmith your question to prompt something beyond a yes-or-no answer. (For example, "Do you run out of groceries in the middle of the week?" should become "When do you typically run out of groceries?" If the customer's answer is "I don't," he'll tell you so.)

This is quite different from the Question of the Week described in Chapter 9. That's a random question, asked of anyone you happen to be in contact with that week, just to keep learning. In that case, you want a very short and consistent answer so you can later search, for example, your trouble, ticketing system for responses.

For this question, you're choosing specific customers you trust and asking them (in individual emails) to elaborate on the question so that your team doesn't waste time arguing over unproven opinions.

Questions for an Existing Product

When you have existing products, both you and your customers may have some preconceived notions to overcome. Customers may have seen a previous product roadmap presentation and be expecting certain features. You may have your own biases about what you think customers need and want.

When you use [our product], what's the first thing you do with it?

The situation

You'd like to learn more about customers' subjective experience. Procedural questions sometimes get you a more detailed answer.

What you'll learn

Depending on how you measure your product usage, you may get the factual answer to this question from your quantitative analytics. I'm often surprised, though, by how frequently a customer's subjective recollection of what she does differs from our objective logging of the actions she takes.

What's the most useful thing that you regularly do with our product?

The situation

You have a hypothesis about what customers value the most. You'd like to validate it to determine where to invest in improving your product.

What you'll learn

People who build products tend to believe that customers will derive the most value from the most difficult or technologically advanced features. This is often not true! I've often heard customers explain that the most used and useful features relate to easy actions like sharing or exporting.

If you had [requested feature] today, how would that make your life better?

The situation

A customer has just asked for a specific feature or change to your product. Maybe you don't think it's aligned with your product vision or maybe you just aren't sure you understand what the customer is asking for.

You may need to adjust the level of language formality, depending on your customers and your existing relationship. There's a small risk of customers perceiving this question as glib or dismissive. I do recommend keeping it deliberately personal and vague, though—"make your life better" or "make your job easier." If you ask about something more specific, like saving time or money, you'll get a more constrained answer.

What you'll learn

The problem that this customer is trying to solve!

Other customers have told me that they experience [problem]…

The situation

As a last resort question in a customer development interview. If you are trying to validate that a problem affects other customers, it's a stronger signal if someone mentions the problem unprompted. But sometimes you have a strong intuition: you just *know* this customer experiences a problem, even though she hasn't mentioned it yet. When this happens, a nudge may help get her talking.

When you don't have time for an extended interview. You can also use this question if you don't have enough time for an extended interview, in which case it serves as a useful standalone conversation starter. (Note that it's not a yes/no question but an invitation for the customer to start talking.)

When you see a pattern and want to challenge it. As patterns begin to emerge, you can use this question by stating the opposite of the pattern and claiming that mythical other people do it another way. See Chapter 6 for details.

What you'll learn

For some reason, the mention of other customers seems to trigger people to give more thoughtful, honest responses than blind agreement or disagreement.

This may be because it is perceived as being granted permission to complain. Those of you who've been on the other end of an angry customer phone call may find this hard to believe, but most customers don't actually feel comfortable complaining, which means that their problems go unresolved.

Using a Storytelling Demo

Sometimes asking a question is not as effective as telling a story and inviting comments.

Here's an excerpt from a demo script that I used at Yammer to get customer responses to some new feature concepts:

I'd like to walk you through how we envision one of your employees working with Yammer. We're definitely looking for your feedback, so please feel free to comment and ask questions as I go.

- - - - -

So we're going to start with your fictional employee, Jessica, who is an employee of the fictional company, Alpine Style. Jessica is supporting sales staff who are at a conference this week.

```
[load first page of demo, displaying logged-
in view of Yammer]

[scroll down to the conversation posted by
"Brian" about contacts at REI]
```

Now Jessica is reading the conversations posted by other employees at Alpine Style. She'll see that someone is asking a question that she can help with. Now, in this case, Brian, who initiated this conversation on Yammer, wouldn't have known that Jessica could help. If he'd just sent an email, it would've gone to another person and Jessica wouldn't have the opportunity to respond. So now she's going to respond...

```
[type Jessica's response, "We worked with
Mary Stevens before. Let me get her phone
number."]
```

Then Jessica remembers a document that the team used in a past deal with REI, so she navigates to the group to find it.

```
[click on lefthand sidebar menu to advance
the demo to the next screen, which shows
the West Coast Sales group]
```

Now Jessica is looking at the West Coast Sales group, and she can browse the files here...

```
[click on the Files tab to advance the demo
to the next screen, which shows a listing
of files]
```

Jessica sees the file she wants and realizes she has a question for the person who originally put it together. She doesn't have to switch away from this screen and lose focus—she can actually ask a question from right here...

```
[click on the Online Now menu to advance to
the next demo screen, where we show a list
of people who are currently online]

[click on "Rick Chan" to advance to the
next demo screen, which shows a chat com-
pose window]
```

Jessica asks Rick her question about the previous REI deal...

```
[type Jessica's question "Rick, can you help
Brian McConnell with his REI visit tomor-
row?" and click to advance the demo to the
next screen]
```

- - - - -

The storytelling demo puts the focus on the problem that you are trying to solve for your customer instead of on showing them features.

In my experience, customers are likely to correct your demo ("That's not how we'd handle that situation. Let me tell you how..."), which is exactly the kind of information you're seeking in customer development.

If It Works, Keep Asking It

I've provided these questions to ensure that you have a good foundation for both your structured customer development interviews and any ad hoc incremental customer conversations you have. However, you'll find that you won't need this list for long. Once you've started talking to customers regularly, you'll develop a good sense for which types of questions get customers talking. If you asked a question spontaneously and it elicited a five-minute enthusiastic response, by all means keep asking it!

Index

A

Abramson, Mark, 122–123
abstracting up one level, in interview questioning, 67
action items, turning insights into, 115
active listening, 93
actual vs. aspirational responses, in interview questioning, 70
Aetna
  defining MVP at, 153
  Healthagen Strategy Group, 170–172
alternate domains, testing prototypes using alternate, 152
Alvarez, Cindy, 155
Amazon, success rate of tested features, 8
Ariely, Dan, 158
asking for introductions, finding customers by, 35–37
aspirational vs. actual responses, in interview questioning, 70
aspirational vs. real wants, 109–111
assumptions, identifying
  about, 18–19
  making wrong assumptions when, 119
  using business model canvas for, 21
  using list of triggers for, 19–20

Audience Building MVP, 135–137
  case study, 136
  use case, 136–137
author email, 193

B

Balsamiq, creating sketches for prototypes or demos, 152
behavior, best predictor of future, 111
bias
  introducing, 120, 167
  recognizing, 190
Bing Offers, as Other People's Product MVP case study, 145–146
Blank, Steve
  definition of earlyvangelists, 32
  The Four Steps to the Epiphany, xi, 3, 5
  Lean LaunchPad course, 43–44
  on startups on Day Ono, 153
  on survival of business plans, 20
  on testing products, 131
  using business model canvas, 21
blog posts, finding customers using, 44–45
broken or missing links, on websites, 151
bugs (errors), fixing, 189
Build-Measure-Learn feedback loop, 9–10

G

generic parts technique, 73
Geus, Arie de, 149
Gmail, using Rapportive plug-in, 53
Google AdWords, finding customers
    using, 47
Google Docs, using for customer
    development, 112
Google Search
    finding blogs using, 45
    researching interview information
        on, 195
Gosling, Marcus, 135
Gourville, John, 160
Graham, Paul, 59, 163
Gur-esh, Ethan, 155

H

Hagel, John, III, 8
halo effect, bias as, 167
Healthagen Strategy Group, 170–172
helping others makes us happy, as
    motivation, 33
hierarchy of needs (Maslow), 34
Horoszowski, Mark, 38
Hotmail.com, 167
Hotwire, 23
Hotwire, as Single Use Case MVP case
    study, 142–144
Howard, Daniel J., 120
"how disappointed" questions,
    158–159
hypothesis
    changing initial, 119
    interpreting interview responses to
        prove, 108–109
    invalidated, indications of, 119
    over communicating to customers
        impact on, 163–164
    real vs. aspirational wants, 109–111
    turning products into, 22–23
    validated
        about, 108
        components of, 117
        for impossible to reach markets,
            122–123
        recognizing, 127–129
    writing problem, 22–24
hypothesis-driven development, 155
hypothesis testing, in customer
    development, 2

I

identifying assumptions
    about, 18–19
    making wrong assumptions when,
        119
    using business model canvas for, 21
    using list of triggers for, 19–20
IM (Instant Messaging), conducting
    customer interviews using, 51
impact of customer development,
    sharing, 192–193
impossible to reach markets,
    validating, 122–123
incognito customer development,
    167–169
incubation approach, rapid business,
    170–172
inMails, on LinkedIn, 39
innovation adoption lifecycle, 25–26
The Innovator's Dilemma
    (Christensen), 63–64
in-person conversations
    in neutral location, 49–50
    visiting home or office of
        customers, 48–49
Instant Messaging (IM), conducting
    customer interviews using, 51
interface complaints, 188–189
interviews
    abstracting up one level in, 67
    conducting customer
        neutral location in-person
            conversations, 49–50
        over phone, 50
        using instant messaging, 51
        using video chat, 50
        visiting home or office, 48–49
    constraints holding customers back
        in, 71–76
    crafting during conversation
        questions in, 195
    creating interview template, 85–86
    creating summaries of, 112–113
    discovering what customer in
        already doing, 66–71
    eliciting subjective and personal
        answers, 78–79
    emotion at, 85
    emphasizing the personal in, 89
    first
        about, 81–82
        avoiding leading questions, 93
        avoiding product specifics, 99

Mirenda, Kristen, 142–144
missing or broken links, on websites, 151
money, giving, vs. volunteering time, 33
motivating people, 32–35
MVP (Minimum Viable Product)
    about, 131–132
    adapting to existing customers, 150–157
    case studies
        Audience Building, 136
        Concierge, 137–138
        distinguishing between minimum and comprehensive features, 154–155
        Other People's Product, 145–146
        Pre-Order, 135
        Single Use Case, 142–144
        Wizard of Oz, 139–141
    goal of, 132
    interview process and developing, 126
    KISSmetrics, 11–12, 125
    meaning of viable in, 141
    timeline for starting, 107
    types of
        about, 133–134
        Audience Building, 135–137
        Concierge, 137–139
        Other People's Product, 144–146
        Pre-Order, 134–135
        Single Use Case, 141–144
        Wizard of Oz, 139–141
    use cases for types of
        Audience Building, 136–137
        Concierge, 139
        Other People's Product, 146
        Pre-Order, 135
        Single Use Case, 144
        Wizard of Oz, 141
    use cases, stopping at minimum, 154–155

N

NDAs (nondisclosure agreements), 165
Netflix, success rate of tested features, 8
Net Promoter Score, 159
neutral location in-person conversations, 49–50
nondisclosure agreements (NDAs), 165

no-shows, to scheduled interviews, 57
notes, interview
    creating interview template, 85–86
    inviting note taker, 86
    keeping in one file, 111–112
    keeping organized, 111
    taking great, 84–86
    vs. recording, 83–84

O

objections to customer development, responding to, 12–14
O'Malley, Grace, 72
ongoing customer development
    about, 181–182
    clarifying feature requests, 187–188
    closing the loop, 112–113, 190–193
    fixing errors or bugs, 189
    for functionality or design issues, 188–189
    getting help from people already talking to customers, 182–187
    picking standard question of week, 189–190
    recognizing bias, 190
    underutilization of customer support professionals, 185–187
on-site interviews, 49
open-ended questions, responding to customer with, 61, 69, 109
Osterwalder, Alexander (Business Model Generation), 21
"other people do this" statement, 120
Other People's Product MVP, 144–146
    case study, 145–146
    use case, 146
outcomes, focusing on procedures not, 68–69
Outlook email client, changing look and feel of, 167
Outlook Social Connector, 54

P

pair interviewing, 87, 112, 114
Palantir, interaction with customers, 184
patterns, challenging emerging, 120
Pennig, Rachel, 187
personas, in user research, 166

Learn from experts.
Find the answers you need.

Sign up for a **10-day free trial** to get **unlimited access** to all of the content on Safari, including Learning Paths, interactive tutorials, and curated playlists that draw from thousands of ebooks and training videos on a wide range of topics, including data, design, DevOps, management, business—and much more.

Start your free trial at:

oreilly.com/safari

(No credit card required.)

Lightning Source UK Ltd.
Milton Keynes UK
UKOW01f1557070917
308766UK00005B/10/P